CY
NORTH
LE

GREA...

HUGH HALPIN, from Dublin, is a retired engineer who has also worked as a tour guide. A member of Cycling Ireland, he has served as secretary of Skerries Cycling Initiative and is the author of several cycling guides.

Advice to Readers

Every effort is made by our authors to ensure the accuracy of our guidebooks. However, changes can occur after a book has been printed, including changes to rights of way. If you notice discrepancies between this guidebook and the facts on the ground, please let us know, either by email to enquiries@collinspress.ie or by post to The Collins Press, West Link Park, Doughcloyne, Wilton, Cork, T12 N5EF, Ireland.

Acknowledgements

The pleasure of cycling these routes was made all the better in good company. Consequently, my thanks to Brian McNally, Pat Noone, Peter McNally and my son Colin whose inspiration, good humour and patience in front of the camera were much appreciated. Thanks also to my very patient wife, Áine, whose support and encouragement kept me on the road.

CYCLING NORTH LEINSTER

GREAT ROAD ROUTES

LEABHARLANN
CO. CHILL DARA

HUGH HALPIN

The Collins Press

First published in 2018 by
The Collins Press
West Link Park
Doughcloyne
Wilton
Cork
T12 N5EF
Ireland

A CIP record for this book is available from the British Library.

Paperback ISBN: 978-1-84889-345-0

Design and typesetting by Fairways Design
Typeset in Myriad Pro
Printed in Turkey by Imakofset

Photographs
Page 1: Drogheda Boyne Viaduct, County Louth; *pages 2–3*: Bective Abbey, County Meath.

Contents

Routes

Map of Route Start Points

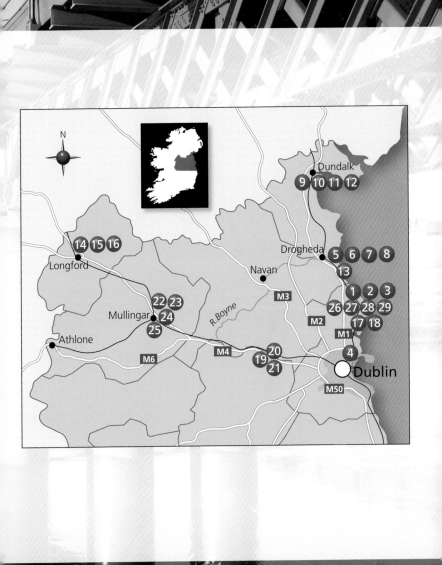

Quick-Reference Route Table

No.	Route	Distance (KM)	Time (Hours)	Grade
1	Balbriggan–Bellewstown Loop	43	2¼–2¾	3
2	Balbriggan–Drogheda Loop	47	2¼–2¾	2
3	Balbriggan–Trim Loop	109	5–5½	3
4	Clontarf–Malahide One Way	35	1½–2	2
5	Drogheda–Clogherhead Loop	41	2–2½	2
6	Drogheda–Kells Loop	93	4½–5	4
7	Drogheda–Monasterboice Loop	32	1½–2	2
8	Drogheda–Slane Loop	44	2–2½	2
9	Dundalk–Annagassan Loop	76	3¾–4¼	2
10	Dundalk–Ardee Loop	64	3–3½	2
11	Dundalk–Castleblaney Loop	81	4–4½	3
12	Dundalk–Flagstaff Loop	68	3–4	4
13	Laytown–Navan Loop	75	3½–4	2
14	Longford–Ballymahon Figure of Eight	56	2½–3¼	3
15	Longford–Cloondara Circuit	36	1¾–2¼	1
16	Longford–Lake Gowna Figure of Eight	69	3½–4	4
17	Lusk–Balrothery Loop	29	1½–1¾	1
18	Lusk–Garristown Loop	42	2–2½	2
19	Maynooth–Athboy Loop	110	5–6	3
20	Maynooth–Edenderry Figure of Eight	96	4½–5	3
21	Maynooth–Tara Loop	75	3½–4	2
22	Mullingar–Abbeyshrule (Royal Canal West) Figure of Eight	55	2¾–3¼	2
23	Mullingar–Athlone (Old Rail Trail) Figure of Eight	95	4½–5	3
24	Mullingar–Lilliput Loop	59	2¾–3¼	2
25	Mullingar–Meath border (Royal Canal East) Figure of Eight	57	3–3½	2
26	Skerries–Bog of the Ring Loop	28	1¼–1¾	1
27	Skerries–Castlebellingham Loop	131	6–7	4
28	Skerries–Donabate Loop	54	2½–3	2
29	Skerries–Rogerstown Estuary Loop	24	1–1½	1

Gain (m)	Score	Traffic	Train Station	Grid Reference	Page Number
412	***	2	Balbriggan	O 202 639	17
325	***	3	Balbriggan	O 202 639	22
455	****	2	Balbriggan	O 202 639	27
291	****	3	Clontarf Road	O 181 362	32
207	****	2	Drogheda MacBride	O 098 748	37
693	****	2	Drogheda MacBride	O 098 748	42
312	****	2	Drogheda MacBride	O 098 748	47
322	****	2	Drogheda MacBride	O 098 748	52
322	***	2	Dundalk Clarke	J 041 069	57
307	****	2	Dundalk Clarke	J 041 069	62
512	***	2	Dundalk Clarke	J 041 069	67
619	****	2	Dundalk Clarke	J 041 069	72
308	****	2	Laytown	O 162 713	77
278	***	2	Longford	N 134 749	82
59	***	1	Longford	N 134 749	87
639	***	2	Longford	N 134 749	92
144	****	2	Rush/Lusk	O 231 538	97
220	***	2	Rush/Lusk	O 231 538	102
233	**	2	Maynooth	N 938 373	107
187	***	2	Maynooth	N 938 373	112
342	***	2	Maynooth	N 938 373	117
118	***	2	Mullingar	N 433 527	122
428	***	1	Mullingar	N 433 527	127
280	***	2	Mullingar	N 433 527	132
139	***	1	Mullingar	N 433 527	137
198	***	2	Skerries	0 246 598	141
735	***	2	Skerries	0 246 598	145
190	***	2	Skerries	0 246 598	151
152	***	2	Skerries	0 246 598	156

Termonfeckin Bridge, County Louth.

Introduction

It's hard to beat cycling on a quiet country road on a pleasant day. A panoramic view, a thrush in song, the smell of freshly mown hay or a caressing breeze rouse the senses to a higher plane. Pedal to the top of a hill and reap the reward of a stunning view and the exhilarating freewheel down the other side. Stop at a Stone Age passage grave or a medieval castle and experience living history. Cycling offers a journey of discovery at a pace to enjoy. After the cycle, the sense of invigoration and physical tiredness, though a contradiction, works, because you feel so good and dinner will taste like a master chef cooked it.

In Ireland, bicycles have grown in popularity in recent years, due in large part to the tax incentive of the Cycle To Work scheme introduced in 2009. The CSO National Travel Survey in 2014 recorded 1.6 per cent of the adult population journeyed by bicycle. We have a long way to go when compared to the Netherlands where 25 per cent of commuting trips were by bicycle in the same year. An interesting statistic is that when more people cycle, there are fewer cycling accidents. A safer cycling environment and earnest promotion by the authorities will encourage more, both young and old, to enjoy the bike. The physical and mental health benefits of regular cycling are well recognised. It is a low-impact activity and can be as intense as you like.

North Leinster has much to offer the cyclist, from numerous meandering, quiet roads and striking scenery to 5,000 years of history and legend in Ireland's Ancient East. Explore coastal, lake, river and canal routes through the rolling landscape of north Dublin, Meath, Westmeath and Longford or take a challenge through the mountains of the breathtaking Cooley Peninsula in Louth. Greenways are on the increase and provide safe, easy routes, ideal for novices and families. After pedalling the miles, there are numerous towns and villages where charming coffee shops and traditional pubs flourish, in which to rest and replenish.

The routes in this book tend to follow local roads to avoid traffic. They offer an opportunity to explore hidden parts of north Leinster, but only ripple the pool of potential. I hope you enjoy them as much as I did. Have a great time and safe cycling!

How to use this book

The book should satisfy the leisure and tourist cyclist wanting to explore the scenic and the curious in this ancient part of Ireland. Those striving for fitness will find the routes helpful to vary training and increase fitness levels by starting on the easier routes and working up. Families may choose to select route segments that are easy to cycle and low in traffic volume. The greenway, canal and rail cycle tracks are particularly suited to family cycling.

There are twenty-nine day-cycling routes varying in distance and elevation, and starting and finishing at railway stations. All but one begin and end at the same railway station. Each route description begins with a brief summary and a table describing the characteristics of the route. An explanation of the table is given below.

An outline map and an elevation chart for each route are provided, followed by the main body of text giving detailed directions and local anecdotes. The directions are in bold text and anecdotes in regular text. This should help make it easy to follow directions without having to read through the anecdotes or vice versa. The anecdotes may prove entertaining while off the bike. Many are embellished tales from the National Folklore Schools Collection and from antiquarian books stored on Ask About Ireland and Internet Archive. These websites are under Useful Contacts below.

Table Explanation

Distance (km)	Total distance of the route
Cycling time (hours)	Time on the bike to cover the distance and based on a reasonable level of adult fitness
Grade	Difficulty of a route based on distance and sum of hill ascents or gain. Routes are graded 1–4, with 4 the most difficult.
	1: Under 40km and/or under 200m
	2: 40–80km and/or 200–400m
	3: 80–120km and/or 400–600m
	4: Over 120km and/or over 600m
Gain	Sum of hill ascents in metres. Downhill not included.
Score	Scenery, heritage and flora and fauna on route. Score is subjective, ranging from 2 to 4 stars.
	2 stars: Pleasant

Score *(cont'd)*	3 stars: Eye-catching
	4 stars: Impressive
Traffic	Traffic volume (graded 1 to 4) is based on the overall route and may be subject to some busy sections.
	1: Little or none
	2: Sporadic
	3: Regular
	4: Heavy
Railway Station	Start and finish location
Grid reference	Irish Mapping Grid reference for railway station

Bikes on trains

InterCity Trains

All InterCity trains have bicycle carriage facilities. On the Dublin–Belfast line, the storage area is separate from the passenger compartment. For all other InterCity routes, the bicycle spaces are within the passenger compartment. Trains are restricted to two bicycles per service and pre-booking is advised. Covered folding bikes can be carried on all services free of charge.

Commuter and DART Trains

Bicycles are permitted on commuter and DART services between 09:30 and 16:00 and after 19:00, Monday to Friday and all day Saturday and Sunday. Currently, there is no charge. Customers are requested to stay with their bicycles in the vestibules. At certain times (e.g. major sporting fixtures/concerts), it may not be possible to carry bicycles. Covered folding bikes can be carried at any time.

Before travelling, check with Irish Rail for any restrictions and charges that may apply. See Useful Contacts below for the Iarnród Eireann (Irish Rail) website.

Climate

Ireland's climate is mild, moist and changeable, with rain and wind common. Temperatures are not extreme; warm summers and mild winters are the norm. The climate is warmer than other areas on the same latitude because the North Atlantic Drift has a temperate effect on the country all year round. North Leinster tends to be drier than other parts of the country, though it can be cooler than the south.

The meteorological office, Met Éireann, gives forecasts of up to five days for weather, wind and temperature. The rainfall radar chart forecasts rain almost in real time and is useful for deciding whether to go cycling in the immediate term. See Useful Contacts below for the Met Éireann website.

Tips

Safety

- A bike needs to be roadworthy and the rider clearly seen night and day. If you are unsure, get the bike checked and have a look at the wide variety of reflective gear and lighting available.
- Stick to the rules of the road. Cyclists can be fined on the spot for failing to observe them.
- Stay behind large turning vehicles. The drivers may not see you in their mirrors and that can be deadly.
- Beware of parked cars in case a door opens unexpectedly in your path.
- Helmets are not compulsory in Ireland though the Road Safety Authority recommends wearing one. However, bicycle helmets are designed only for low-speed impacts, when fitted and worn properly. They are not expected to provide significant protection from a collision with a motor vehicle.
- When a slow-moving vehicle overtakes, be aware of traffic that may be following.
- Keep a distance from the kerb. A high kerb could catch the downstroke of the pedal and throw a cyclist off balance.
- On roads and greenways, respect other users. Signal audibly if approaching a pedestrian or slower cyclist from behind.
- Be confident on the road. Give clear hand signals and position for a turning manoeuvre in plenty of time.
- When cycling in windy conditions, be careful when passing open gaps as a gust, funnelled through the gap, could blow a cyclist off balance.
- Beware of potholes, especially those close to verges that require swerving into traffic to avoid. After rain, deep potholes can be disguised as shallow pools.
- In winter, road surfaces may be greasy even after a dry spell. In particular, slow down when making a turn and on roundabouts.
- Dizziness is a signal that food is needed and a headache is a sign of dehydration. Don't let it get that far.

Other

- To avoid punctures, ensure tyres are pumped to the recommended pressure imprinted on the wall of the tyres. A floor pump with a pressure gauge is a useful accessory to have at home.

- Carry a hand pump, spare tube, a puncture repair kit and tyre levers. At the side of the road, it's easier to replace a tube than fix a puncture. However, if unfortunate enough to get a second puncture, the repair kit is at hand.

- Be aware of the two 'H's: hills and headwind. When cycling distances, it helps to start out against the wind, returning with it on your back. Similarly with hills, get the hills out of the way first. No one wants to push a headwind or steep hill on the way back from a long trip.

- There may be times when dogs give chase. If outpacing the dog is not an option, a stern voice may work, otherwise dismount and put the bike between you and the dog. Move away slowly, while avoiding direct eye contact, and hope for the best.

Gear

There is a wide selection of bicycles to choose from nowadays. Generally road, touring and hybrid bikes are suited to these routes. Having said that, the surface on some roads and segments of greenways can be rough, making riding a little uncomfortable on bikes with the thin, high-pressure tyres fitted to road bikes and some hybrids.

To follow the routes in this book, it is handy to know what distance has been covered. Recording distance, and performance generally, adds enjoyment and competition to cycling. Even when cycling alone one can try to beat a previous performance. Bicycle computers range from those providing basic information to those that also track a route on a map. Smartphones can be used too, as there are several GPS cycling apps available for download. However, keep in mind that GPS will drain the battery more quickly.

Layers of clothing are the recommended way to remain comfortable. A base layer next to the skin, followed by a cycling jersey, winter cycling jacket and gloves are generally enough for winter. A jersey should suffice in summer, with a light jacket if necessary. Padded pants in winter and shorts in summer take care of below the waistline. Overshoes will help keep feet dry and warm in winter.

There are plenty of bicycle bags to choose from for carrying repair equipment, clothing, food, drink and mobile phone for emergencies. Bags range from small saddlebags to side panniers mounted on racks. There are neat backpacks too, though they cause more sweat on the back. Bikes are usually equipped with one or two bottle cages. Two water bottles are recommended for all-day cycling, especially in warm weather. A hydration pack, worn like a backpack, is another option.

Useful Contacts

Emergency services   999 or 112

Cycling and Safety
Governing Body for Cycling in Ireland   www.cyclingireland.ie
The Irish Cycling Advocacy Network   http://cyclist.ie
RSA (Road Safety Advice)   www.rsa.ie

History, Heritage and Folklore
Online publications of local studies   www.askaboutireland.ie
Resource on Ireland's Ancient East   www.irelandsancienteast.com
National Folklore Collection   www.duchas.ie
Internet Archive – online library   https://archive.org/index.php

Mapping
Find a grid reference   www.gridreference.ie
Find a location using a grid reference   irish.gridreferencefinder.com

Rail Transport
Irish Rail   www.irishrail.ie

Weather
Met Éireann (Irish met. office)   www.met.ie

1. Balbriggan-to-Bellewstown Loop

Balbriggan – Stamullen – Bellewstown – Naul – Balbriggan

Distance (km): 43	**Score:** ✳ ✳ ✳
Cycling Time (hours): 2¼–2¾	**Traffic:** 2
Grade: 3	**Train Station:** Balbriggan
Gain: 412m	**Grid Reference:** O 202 639

This is a good workout with several hills to keep you sprightly. The route passes through rural Fingal and Meath, with fine views and charming villages to make your day. Horse racing at Bellewstown can be traced back to 1726 and is still going on.

Cycling through Balscaddan from Balbriggan, County Dublin.

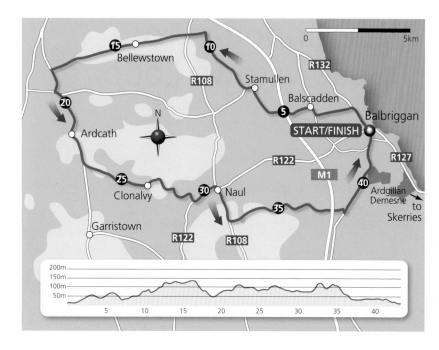

On leaving Balbriggan train station, turn right, followed by a left that will take you to a junction with the main street near traffic lights. Turn right; there is no signpost, however it is the Drogheda direction. Continue to a cycle track on the left. Follow the track, passing sixteenth-century Bremore Castle on the right. It was originally built by the Barnewall family and is now being restored. At the end of the cycle track, turn left onto Flemington Lane and continue to the top. Turn right at the T-junction here, following the sign for Balscaddan. Soon after, take the left, following another sign for Balscaddan.

Balscadden village gets its name from the Irish, *Baile na Scadán* or 'town of the herrings'. You might wonder how you could catch a herring here since it's far from the sea. Local tradition has it that herrings were once transported inland from a small port in Balscadden Bay, also known as Cromwell's Harbour. The fish were prepared in the village for the Dublin market. Of course, this could just be a red herring.

Cycle through Balscaddan and cross the M1 motorway. Continue to a T-junction. Turn right towards Stamullen and enjoy the coastal view to the right. Descend to a T-junction near the village. Turn left and cycle to a nearby junction with two turns to the right. Take the rightmost one, not signposted, and follow the road passing the Benedictine priory at

View near Bellewstown Racecourse, County Meath

Silverstream, about 9km from Balbriggan. Arrive at a junction with a sign for Bellewstown. Turn left to follow the sign and continue straight on through a crossroads to Bellewstown. There is a steady climb to the racecourse where you can enjoy the panoramic views. Bellewstown is about 15km from the start.

Michael Collier, the notorious highway robber, was born in 1780 in Bellewstown. He worked the north road from Dublin. One of his more famous exploits was a plan to rob the Dublin–Belfast mail coach at Bloody Hollow in Santry. The hardened coach guards were well armed, as were some of the passengers. The odds weren't good for Collier but he needed the money, so he came up with a daring plan. After collecting several old hats and coats, he arranged them along the hedges on each side of the road. When the coach approached, Collier leaped out in front of it while calling on his gang of hats and coats to hold fire unless provoked. The coach came to an abrupt halt in a cloud of dust and neighing horses. Seeing they were surrounded, the guards and passengers delivered up all money and valuables to the highwayman. The next morning, a squad of dragoons, sent from Dublin to arrest him and his bandoleros, came upon the dummy gang. By this time, Collier was well away, planning his next scheme.

Continue through Bellewstown and begin a steep descent. Follow the road all the way to a T-junction. Turn left following the sign for Ardcath, 3km away. Cycle to a crossroads and turn left again to a nearby Y-junction. Keep right and cycle into Ardcath. Continue on the main road through the village to the first crossroads. Turn left here in the direction of Naul and Clonalvy and stay on this road until you arrive in Clonalvy. Pass through the village and arrive at a T-junction where you turn right in the Naul direction. Continue to another T-junction and turn right again over the River Delvin. Continue to the R122 and turn left onto it towards Naul. At the next T-junction, turn right into Naul village. Naul is 31km from Balbriggan.

In 1820, Naul impressed the traveller Thomas Cromwell so much that he described it thus: 'Naul … bordering on the county of Meath, has many charms for the traveller of taste in its very beautiful Glen, whose romantic rocks, cascade, and rugged caves, are finely contrasted by the picturesque ruins of its antique Castle … It will bear comparison even with some of the romantic scenery in the far-famed county of Wicklow.'

Continue through Naul, passing the thatched Seamus Ennis Centre on the left and begin ascending the steep hill out of the village. After the climb, there is a descent to a crossroads. Turn left here onto the L5080, signposted for Belgee. Cycle on to a staggered crossroads while enjoying the coastal view. At the staggered crossroads, turn right and then immediately left. Continue to a T-junction where you turn right

John the Baptist Church, Clonalvy

into the Bog of the Ring (there is no signpost but it is clearly a bog). Cross over the M1 motorway and stay on this road until you meet the junction with the R132. Turn left towards Balbriggan. Continue to Balbriggan and after passing the hollow in the town centre, take the third right turn onto Railway Street to the station.

At the end of the eighteenth century, Balbriggan was thriving. Its local landlord, George Hamilton, was instrumental in developing the pier to accommodate large ships and the textile industries that enriched the town for two centuries after. In 1813, the Rev. James Hall described the build and comfort of the ordinary houses in the town, suggesting the well-being of its inhabitants. He wrote: 'Though the houses in Balbriggan, for the most part, built with mud, and covered with thatch, yet they have a neat appearance, the walls being harled with lime, and the thatch, in general, thick and neatly sewed to the roof. This, with its projecting over the wall, as it were to cover and keep them warm, gives pleasure, and suggests the snug, easy, comfortable state of the inmates.' The reverend would have made a great real estate agent.

Balbriggan Harbour, County Dublin

2. Balbriggan-to-Drogheda Loop

Balbriggan – Stamullen – Drogheda – Mornington – Bettystown – Laytown – Balbriggan

Distance (km): 47	**Score:** ✳ ✳ ✳
Cycling Time (hours): 2¼–2¾	**Traffic:** 3
Grade: 2	**Train Station:** Balbriggan
Gain: 325m	**Grid Reference:** O 202 639

The varied landscape on this route makes it appealing. Cycle by river, sea and countryside, while rolling hills offer some great views. Medieval Drogheda holds many secrets and for those who would like to know more, there is a tourist office in the town centre to help unlock them.

Cadaver stone in St Patrick's Cemetery, Stamullen, County Meath.

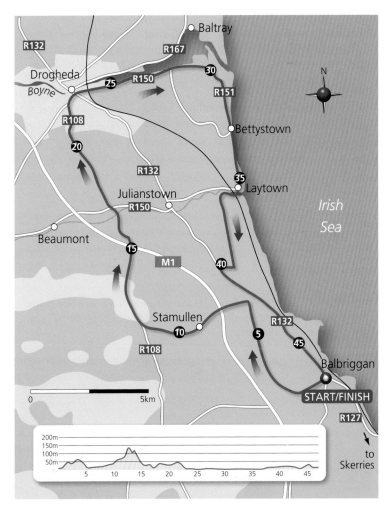

On exiting Balbriggan railway station, turn right and then left to the nearby T-junction at the main street. Turn left again at the T-junction onto the main street and go straight through the set of traffic lights between the Milestone and Harvest pubs. Cycle to the nearby crossroads just before another set of lights and turn right into Clonard Street. Continue to another crossroads and cycle straight across to climb a hill. At the top is a T-junction, turn right and follow the road to yet another crossroads. Continue straight across, following the sign for Gormanstown.

Climb a hill to a water scheme on the right and then descend. The Mourne Mountains can be viewed to the right. At the bottom of the hill, cross a small bridge over the Delvin River; here it's merely a stream. Pass the entrance to Gormanston College, once the demesne of the Viscounts Gormanston. At the next crossroads, which is staggered, turn left following the sign for Stamullen. Cross the M1 motorway and enter Stamullen about 8.5km from Balbriggan station. On the right, opposite the shopping centre, is the old cemetery and church ruins.

In the medieval cemetery at Stamullen lies the burial vault of the Viscounts Gormanston. There is also a macabre image of death, a cadaver stone. This engraved tomb cover depicts the decaying corpse of a woman. There are creepy-crawlies and other unsavoury creatures feeding off the corpse. The dead woman is wearing a headdress with her shroud tied back at the head and feet, presumably to present the grim reality of death. Cadaver stones were fashionable across Europe following the Black Death and other such fatal visitations. They remind us that we are all the same in death, no matter how rich, famous or titled. The Stamullen stone dates to about 1450 and has seen many a funeral in its time.

Continue through Stamullen. On the outskirts is a junction with three roads. Take the middle one, signposted for Bellewstown, and continue up a hill to a junction with the R108. Turn right onto the R108,

Railway viaduct, Drogheda, County Louth.

signposted for Drogheda. Soon after is another junction. Keep right and climb a stiff hill. At the top, there are fine views over the coast and the Irish Sea. The descent is followed by another uphill push. Cycle on to cross over the M1 motorway, about 15km from the start. Continue past Dardistown Castle, a large fifteenth-century manor house, tucked away on the right.

After crossing the River Nanny, arrive at a staggered crossroads. Turn left followed by a right towards Drogheda, staying on the R108. Push on to a crossroads and cycle straight across in the direction of Drogheda, 3km away. Cross under the Navan railway line to a set of traffic lights and continue straight through. Follow the road as it veers to the right and descend a hill to another set of traffic lights. Turn left and then right towards Drogheda town centre at the next traffic lights. Ahead is St Mary's Bridge over the River Boyne. Don't cross it; rather, turn right before the bridge. Drogheda is about 22.5km from Balbriggan.

There is a place in Drogheda called Hardman's Gardens after a well-to-do family who lived in the town. A rather gruesome tale is told about one, Anne Hardman. She died in 1884 and was interred in a tomb at the Anglican church, St Peter's. She was accompanied by her copious jewellery, which did not go unnoticed by her servants, one of whom decided to collect his pension early. On the night of her burial, he broke into the tomb and began filling his pockets. He was about to leave when his greedy eyes fell upon the rings adorning Mrs Hardman's fingers. Having tried and failed to pull off the stubborn jewellery, he produced a knife. As the sawing progressed, he failed to realise that a corpse does not spurt blood. Suddenly, Anne Hardman rose up, shrieking like a demented spirit. Blood drained from the servant's face and his hair turned white. He fled the country. Meanwhile, Anne Hardman had great difficulty in convincing her relatives she was actually alive. She lived for another twenty years before returning to the same tomb. Is she still there? Why not check it out at St Peter's!

Cycle on, following the south bank of the River Boyne towards Mornington on the R150. In Mornington, the road becomes the R151 and it eventually turns to the right. The distance cycled so far is about 29km. If you divert left at this turn, the Maiden Tower and Lady's Finger come into view.

There are various versions of a tale about how these two tall structures got their names. This is one of them: a young lady fell in love with a sailor, but he wasn't sure if he felt the same. He went to sea after promising to make up his mind on the voyage. Before leaving, he told her that on his return if his ship flew a flag with a heart, it meant he loved her. However, if the ship's flag had a broken heart, he did not. She waited faithfully for five long years, each day climbing the Maiden Tower to see if her sailor's ship was on the horizon. Finally, she saw it approach. She strained to see the flag and when it finally came into view, she saw a broken heart on the fluttering cloth. The young lady was so distraught that she threw herself off the Maiden Tower but rather than be killed, she broke a finger. Meanwhile, the sailor had second thoughts and, after finding out what happened, he built the Lady's Finger to prove his love. He gave up the sea and became a successful insurance broker and she never had to climb the Maiden Tower again. However, he had her insured, just in case.

From the turn to the Maiden Tower and Lady's Finger, continue on the R151 out of Mornington to a junction where you veer left, staying on the main road towards Bettystown, 3km away. Keep right at the next junction, remaining on the main road. Cycle into the centre of Bettystown, where the R151 merges with the R150. Continue to Laytown, home to beach horse racing since 1868. There are good views south along the coast to Skerries.

The road eventually veers right to a car park and a footbridge crossing the River Nanny. Cross the footbridge and turn right under the green railway bridge and follow the road by the river, heading upstream. The road then turns south away from the Nanny. Continue straight on to the third right-hand turn. The turn is nearly 40km from the railway station. Take this right-hand turn and cycle to the T-junction with the R132. Turn left onto the R132, signposted for Balbriggan. Keep left at the nearby V-junction to avoid heading to the M1. Continue to Balbriggan and, on the outskirts, passing Bremore Castle on the left (being renovated at the time of writing). Cycle to the centre of town and through the traffic lights sandwiched by the Milestone and Harvest pubs. Then take the next left onto Railway Street to the station.

River Nanny estuary, Laytown, County Meath.

3. Balbriggan-to-Trim Loop

Balbriggan – Garristown – Trim – Navan – Kentstown – Duleek – Julianstown – Balbriggan

Distance (km): 109	Score: ✷ ✷ ✷ ✷
Cycling Time (hours): 5–5½	Traffic: 2
Grade: 3	Train Station: Balbriggan
Gain: 455m	Grid Reference: O 202 639

Plenty of heritage on this route, especially from the medieval period, though the distance will limit the number of stops. Hilly sections are undertaken early to allow an easy return journey. Views are particularly good at Skreen (Skryne) and look across the legendary Hill of Tara.

Medieval church ruin at Garristown.

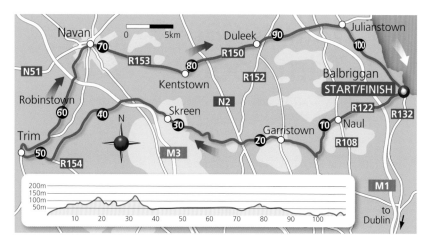

On exiting Balbriggan train station, turn right and then left. Continue the short distance to the T-junction onto the main street and turn left to the traffic lights. At the lights, turn right onto the R122 towards Naul, home of the great uilleann piper Seamus Ennis. Continue on this road all the way to Naul, passing over the M1 motorway en route. At the junction in the centre of Naul by the thatched Seamus Ennis Cultural Centre, turn right onto the R108 signposted for Drogheda and, soon after, turn left onto the R122, following the sign for Garristown.

Continue on the R122 for about 13km and then turn right onto the R130, signposted for Garristown. Continue to the T-junction in the centre of Garristown and turn right onto the L1006, signposted for Duleek. Take the next left nearby towards Navan, passing the old church ruins. Continue to the crossroads at the N2 and cross it onto the L5007. Cycle on to a T-junction at the Snailbox pub and turn left. At the next T-junction, turn right, following the sign for Navan, and then take the nearby left also signposted for Navan. Continue on this road to Skreen (Skryne), where the old church ruins offer great views.

Known locally as Skryne Tower, this fifteenth-century church dominates the Hill of Skryne and can be seen clearly from the Hill of Tara to the west. The church is associated with St Colmcille who founded the monastery at Kells. The name Skreen, in Irish, means Colmcille's shrine. Legend has it that the saint's relics rested in the old church. The carving of a figure can be seen above a doorway on the south side, an image of a bishop, perhaps St Colmcille.

While facing the ruins, take the road to the right and cycle to a T-junction about 22km from the start. Turn left here, following the sign for Navan. Arriving at the next T-junction, turn left again for Navan. Continue to a staggered crossroads at the R147. Cross the R147 onto the L2201 by the pub and continue towards Trim. Pass eighteenth-century Bellinter House hotel or divert to take a look. It was originally built for John Preston and designed by Richard Castle.

After Bellinter, arrive at a crossroads by a pub. Divert right to view the picturesque scene of twelfth-century Bective Abbey by the River Boyne, otherwise continue straight on. Cycle to the junction with the R154 and turn right towards Trim. Arrive at a roundabout and take the second exit. On the right nearby is a flower-filled boat called Liam and a turn to Newtown and the ruins of the Priory of St John the Baptist. However, continue to another roundabout. Take the second exit, following the sign for the town centre. The striking structure of Trim Castle comes into view.

Whatever you do, don't lose your head in Trim. A statute of 1465 gave permission to all men in County Meath to behead anyone found thieving. A thief's decapitated head was brought to the portreeve, or mayor, of Trim. The official would place it on a spear and exhibit the gruesome sight at Trim Castle as a warning to would-be thieves. The beheader was

Bective Abbey, County Meath.

Trim Castle, County Meath.

permitted to levy a charge on every landowner in the barony where the thief was caught, an incentive, perhaps, to behead the odd innocent if stuck for a few bob. The practice of displaying severed heads seems to have been common in Trim. An example in 1452 was Farrell Roe Og, a celebrity chieftain. He was caught and beheaded at a place called Cruach Abhall. His head was first brought to Trim Castle for exhibiting before it was dispatched to Dublin to continue the show. Fortunately, there are less grisly ways of becoming a celebrity these days.

Cycle into the centre of Trim, about 53km from the start. The one-way system will steer you around to the left and to a nearby T-junction. Turn right to cross the River Boyne and follow the one-way system towards 'All Routes'. Arriving at a T-junction, turn left. At the next T-junction, turn right, following the sign for Navan. At a signalled crossroads turn left onto the R161 for Navan. After cycling 57km, take a left-hand turn onto the L40071, signposted for Robinstown. At the staggered crossroads in Robinstown, turn right and then immediately left for Navan. Follow the road to the outskirts of the town and arrive at a signalled T-junction. Turn right onto the L3416, following the sign for the town centre. Cycle through the town centre to a road triangle and keep left, following the sign for all other routes. Arrive at a signalled T-junction and turn right. At the nearby signalled crossroads, turn left over the River Boyne onto the R153 towards Kentstown and Duleek. Continue on the R153 until you reach Kentstown, about 80km from the start.

There was a story told hereabouts of a man who walked from his home in Kentstown to Navan to do some shopping. The dual tasks of walking and shopping took their toll, resulting in a terrible thirst, so he adjourned to a public house to quench it. The thirst was insatiable and he continued to

River Boyne at Navan, County Meath.

imbibe until it was satisfied. The man was in good spirits when he finally took the road back home against a blustery east wind. As he approached home he reached for his pipe and struck several matches to light it. On each attempt, the wind blew the match out. Sensibly, the man put his back to the wind and struck again. On this occasion, the match fired up and he lit his pipe. He stood awhile, drawing on the pipe until it glowed to his satisfaction. Only then did he continue his journey. The realisation hit him as he walked into Navan that he had forgotten to turn back around after lighting his pipe.

At the church in Kentstown, veer left onto the R150 towards Duleek. Continue to the staggered crossroads at the N2. Turn right and immediately left onto the R150 towards Duleek. Continue to Duleek and on entering the village note the church towers to the left. The site entrance is on the left, just past the credit union. The ruins are the remains of twelfth-century St Mary's Abbey and there are many interesting stone crosses and images there. Continue through the town to a staggered crossroads. Turn right and immediately left onto the R150, signposted for Julianstown. Continue to Julianstown, about 98km from the start.

At Julianstown is a T-junction connecting with the R132. Turn right onto it towards Balbriggan. After cycling about 100km, keep left at a Y-junction, following the R132 towards Balbriggan, to avoid the M1 motorway. Continue to Balbriggan and into the centre of town. Cycle straight through the signalled junction, at the earlier turn for Naul, to nearby Railway Street. Turn left onto it to the train station.

4. Clontarf-to-Malahide One Way

Clontarf – Sutton – Howth – Portmarnock – Malahide

Distance (km): 35	**Score:** ✳ ✳ ✳ ✳
Cycling Time (hours): 1½ to 2	**Traffic:** 3
Grade: 2	**Train Station:** Clontarf Road
Gain: 291m	**Grid Reference:** O 181 362

Starting near Dublin city centre, this coastal route admires the features of Dublin Bay and is partly on a cycle track avoiding the busy road. The climb at Howth is rewarded with magnificent views over Dublin Bay, and the beach at Portmarnock is a sandy gem. There is a regular train service back from Malahide.

Mouth of the River Liffey at Clontarf, Dublin.

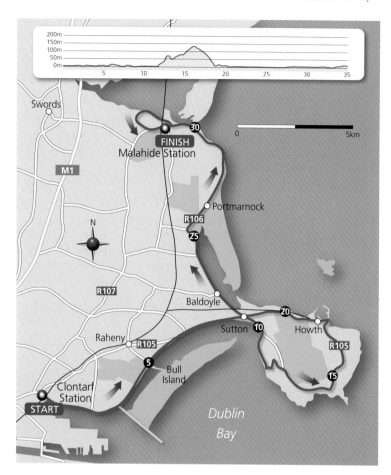

On exiting Clontarf DART station car park, turn right onto the Clontarf Road. At the nearby junction on the seafront, take up the cycle track on the seaward side; there is a sail sculpture beside it. Follow the track running parallel to the Clontarf Road, with extensive views of Dublin Bay and the mouth of the River Liffey. At about 3km from the railway station is the North Bull Wall and Bull Island. It is possible to divert to the end of the Bull Wall, a round trip of about 3km. At the end is a statue dedicated to the Virgin Mary called Realt Na Mara (Star of the Sea).

Thanks to Hollywood, William Bligh became famous, or infamous perhaps, for the mutiny on his ship HMS *Bounty*. Though his personnel skills may not have been up to much, he was an accomplished sailor and navigator. Bligh designed the North Bull Wall facing the already-built South Wall to reduce the silting that had blocked the entrance to the Liffey. His design diverted sand from the mouth of the river to form Bull Island on its north side. Bligh also charted and mapped Dublin Bay. Thanks to him, ships were able to move safely in and out of Dublin port, even at low tide. Today, Bull Island continues to grow, a beacon, if you like, of William Bligh's successful design.

From the North Bull Wall, continue on the track passing St Anne's public park on the left. The Guinness family of brewing fame originally owned it. On the seaward side is a fine view of Howth Head tumbling to the water. The track comes to an end at traffic lights about 9km from the start. Rejoin the road and follow it to nearby Sutton Cross. This is a busy junction, marked by the Marine Hotel over to the right.

Near the Marine Hotel lived an Irish engineer called Bindon Blood Stoney. Like William Bligh, he was associated with developing the River Liffey as a port. Stoney's contribution was to build deep-water quays using precast concrete. To make this possible, he designed a diving bell with enough room inside for six men to work. It went into service in 1871. Once the eighty-ton bell was in position, water was pumped out and air pumped in. The working detail entered through a tunnel from the surface to work on the riverbed. They excavated the sites where the massive concrete blocks would go. The bell was in use to repair dock walls up to 1958 and is now on view at Sir John Rogerson's Quay in Dublin.

Howth Head viewed from Clontarf.

34

Marina at Howth.

Turn right at Sutton Cross, following a sign for Scenic Route. This is the R105, the main road that circles Howth Head from Sutton Cross. Turn right again off the R105 at the nearby church, keeping to the coast. After passing Sutton dinghy club, the road begins to ascend away from the coast into a residential area. Eventually, it comes to a stop sign at Sutton Park School. Turn right and continue up the hill. At about 12km from the start, turn right towards Howth at another stop sign and back on the R105. Continue to the signpost for Summit where you can divert right to admire the magnificent views over Dublin Bay. Otherwise, descend to Howth Harbour and cycle through the buzzing village towards Sutton Cross. On the outskirts of Howth, on the left, is the entrance to Howth Castle.

A story is told of Christopher St Lawrence, the twentieth lord of Howth also known as the 'blind lord'. However, he played deaf to Granuaile, the 'Pirate Queen' from County Mayo, when she knocked on his door, looking for some food after her journey from the Lord Deputy in the city. The castle gate was locked while the lord ate his dinner. An empty stomach can make one do desperate things, so Granuaile kidnapped Lord Howth's son, who happened to be on the beach. The boy was finally returned when Granuaile was given a promise that the gate would never again be locked at dinnertime. She then sailed back to Mayo and returned to the day job of robbing ships.

Returning to Sutton Cross, turn right onto the R106 towards Baldoyle. Continue straight to the T-junction at Baldoyle and turn right towards the fine church of Ss Peter and Paul. There is signpost for Malahide and the R106 at the junction, though it is easy to miss. Continue to a roundabout and take the second exit. Follow the coast road to another roundabout and take the second exit towards

Toots, the Malahide road train, outside Malahide railway station.

Malahide, 6km away. Cycle through Portmarnock, keeping an eye out for a green space on the right. It is a busy hangout for birds. Duck and Brent geese dominate, depending on the time of year. Continue along the coast road till you get to Malahide. While cycling into Malahide, look for the Grand Hotel on the left.

The first petrol-driven car ever to roll onto an Irish road was imported by the medical practitioner and owner of the Grand Hotel, Dr John Colohan. Costing £189, the vehicle was an 1898 Benz Velo Comfortable. Karl Benz, a founding member of the executive car brand Mercedes-Benz, designed and built it. The vehicle was later discovered in a ramshackle state in County Tipperary in 1984. It was lovingly restored to full working order. The 3hp single-cylinder vehicle bears the number IK 52. It was the fifty-second car registered after the registration system was introduced in 1903. It is easy to imagine the doctor's car scattering horse poo all about as it sped along at 25 km/h to a medical emergency. Locals must have yearned for the good old days when speed was more leisurely.

At the signalled crossroads in the centre of Malahide, turn right towards the marina. At the next traffic lights, turn left and continue to the inner estuary on the west side of the railway line. Cycle on, following the road as it veers away from the water's edge at Malahide Yacht club. At the next traffic lights, turn left. Continue to a T-junction at a pedestrian entrance to Malahide Castle and gardens. The picturesque demesne is worth a detour. Turn left at the T-junction and cycle on to cross over the railway bridge by the entrance to the train station. (Regular DART rail services depart for Clontarf during off-peak periods (see page 13). There is no need to book and no charge for a bicycle.)

5. Drogheda-to-Clogherhead Loop

Drogheda – Termonfeckin – Clogherhead – Sandpit – Drogheda

Distance (km): 41

Cycling Time (hours): 2–2½

Grade: 2

Gain: 207m

Score: ✴ ✴ ✴ ✴

Traffic: 2

Train Station: Drogheda MacBride

Grid Reference: O 098 748

The picturesque Boyne Estuary and the panoramic Louth coast get a showing on this route. The Boyne Estuary near Drogheda is a haven for seabirds and Clogherhead has been a popular seaside resort for generations; it's easy to see why.

Drogheda Viaduct, County Louth.

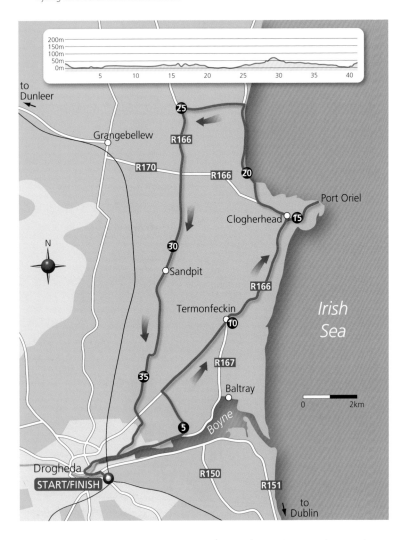

After exiting Drogheda train station car park, continue to the nearby traffic lights and turn right towards the town centre. Cycle to the church of St Mary's; its fine steeple is obvious. Then take the nearby right-hand turn at the traffic lights to cross the River Boyne towards the town centre. Immediately after crossing the bridge, turn right again to follow the river east. Take the second left turn away from the river, followed by the right towards Baltray. Follow the road out of town and under the Boyne Viaduct to meet the river again.

Beaulieu House, Drogheda.

The Boyne Viaduct was constructed to connect the Dublin–Drogheda railway to Belfast. It was a massive feat of engineering and so innovative that the foundations were made of cotton wool, or so it was believed. Some passengers were so nervous they would insist on leaving the train on one side of the bridge, cross the river by a different bridge and catch the train on the other side. The inconvenience turned out to be completely unnecessary. Though cotton wool was used, its purpose was to soak up water that leaked into the cofferdams. These were temporary structures on the riverbed built to prevent work areas being flooded. After the solid foundations were laid, the cotton wool was left in situ, creating the myth. Of course, the myth turned out to be another ball of fluff.

After cycling about 5km from the railway station, turn left away from the river and pass seventeenth-century Beaulieu House. It is open to the public during summer. The property is a striking design built in the Artisan Mannerism style created by masons rather than architects. Continue to a stop sign at a crossroads and turn right, following the sign for the sleepy village of Termonfeckin, 3km away.

Termonfeckin, or Fechin's hut, is named after the seventh-century saint whose name has come to be unfortunately associated with '*that* word'. St Fechin lived at the time of an early famine in Ireland. Legend tells of the hungry high kings imploring the saint to pray for a plague on the common folk to reduce their numbers. The saint did as requested, though it proved God had no favourites for St Fechin caught the plague himself and died. Though this is a tale, the plague itself was real. It reaped havoc around 665 AD, killing large numbers. In more recent times, naming children after saints was popular in Ireland. Fechin, though, was not one of them.

Continue through Termonfeckin and at the top of a hill, keep right on the R166 towards Clogherhead. At a nearby roundabout, take the first exit. While progressing towards Clogherhead, note the vast number of holiday homes below the road near the sea.

Clogherhead was the birthplace of an unusual woman called Jennie Hodgers. Born in 1843, she travelled Ireland with her father, struggling to make a living. To get work, Jennie dressed as a boy. When she grew up, she immigrated to the US and joined the Union army during the American Civil War as Albert Cashier. Albert was somewhat unmanly and the smallest soldier in her company but no one took much notice. War conditions forced soldiers to wear the same clothing day and night for weeks, which allowed Jennie to avoid detection. She fought and survived for three years during the war. After her military career, she settled in Illinois where she continued as Albert and kept very much to herself. Eventually, she ended up in institutional care. It was there that her secret was revealed. Jennie was then forced to live in the women's ward and wear dresses for the first time in fifty years. She died in 1915. However, she was buried with full military honours as was her wish.

In the centre of Clogherhead, 15km from the train station, turn right onto the L6282 towards the harbour at Port Oriel. This 3km detour there and back is worth it for the views of the Mourne and Cooley mountains. After returning from Port Oriel to Clogherhead, turn right onto the R166. Continue in the direction of Dunleer to a church at a crossroads and turn right onto the L6282, signposted for Coast Road. The Mourne

Port Oriel, Clogherhead

and Cooley mountains come into view again. The highest peak nearest the sea is Slieve Donard, the tallest of the Mourne Mountains. The road soon hugs the beach, known locally as the 'Big Strand.' At Lurganboy beach, turn left away from the sea. The road comes to a T-junction; turn left here onto the R166 in the direction of Clogerhead. At the next crossroads, cycle straight on towards Sandpit, leaving behind the R166 as it goes left.

At about 28km from the train station are the remains of a small petrol station at the side of the road, a ghost from the past. The old pump has hands on it rather like a clock (forty-five minutes of petrol, please), very different from the digital displays of today. Continue through the next crossroads and cycle on to Sandpit, a small village with a big church. Sandpit is about 32km from the start.

After Sandpit, follow the signs for Drogheda and, after passing a cemetery, arrive at the nearby crossroads. Cycle straight across onto the L2307, signposted for North Quay. Continue to a stop sign just past Greenhills School. Cycle straight on to a T-junction and turn right along the river and under the Boyne Viaduct. Follow the road while it leaves the river to a crossroads and there turn left near a pub called Ní Cairbre. At the next T-junction, turn right along the quays. Continue following the river upstream to a T-junction and then turn left to cross over the river. At the second set of traffic lights turn left again onto the Dublin Road. Cycle on, passing a petrol station on the way, to traffic lights where you veer left to the train station.

On the road to Sandpit.

6. Drogheda-to-Kells Loop

Drogheda – Collon – Kells – Slane – Drogheda

Distance (km): 93

Cycling Time (hours): 4½–5

Grade: 4

Gain: 693m

Score: ✳ ✳ ✳ ✳

Traffic: 2

Train Station: Drogheda MacBride

Grid Reference: O 098 748

This longer route will stretch your legs and provide an opportunity to visit the original home of the Book of Kells. Another heritage site on the route has a modern twist: since 1981, historic Slane Castle has hosted huge concerts from some of the biggest names in the music business.

Celtic cross at Kells, County Meath.

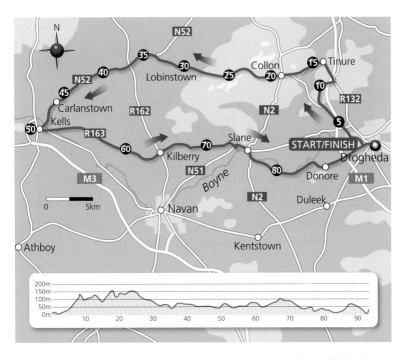

Exit Drogheda train station car park and, at the nearby traffic lights, turn right towards the town centre. Continue to follow the road when it becomes a dual carriageway. After crossing the River Boyne, take the next left-hand turn, following the sign for Navan. Cycle to a roundabout and take the second exit to another roundabout, about 4.5km from the train station. Here, take the second exit onto the L6322, signposted for Hill of Rath. Stay on this road all the way to a T-junction and turn right. The turn is about 10km from the start. Continue until you come to a junction with the R132. Turn left and soon after, take the next left off the R132 towards Tinure. Continue to a roundabout and take the first exit to follow the road to Tinure. At the crossroads in the centre of the village, turn left to Collon and continue all the way there.

Collon is associated with the Foster family who came to County Louth in the 1600s. Originally tenant farmers, they became significant landowners and members of the Ango-Irish ascendancy. John Foster was the last Speaker of the Irish House of Commons when he wound it up in August 1800. Born in 1740 Speaker Foster enjoyed a very successful political career as MP for Dunleer and County Louth. Foster was considered an ardent supporter of the Irish government in Britain and a great debater using his 'articulate' if 'grating' voice to score points. He was a champion of Irish economic

Headfort Bridge on the R163 near Kells.

improvement to counter the threat to the Anglo-Irish ascendancy. He was also the ascendancy's most effective spokesman against Catholic Emancipation. He lived a long life for those days, departing around his 88th year.

At the crossroads in the centre of Collon, cycle straight across onto the L1297 towards Lobinstown. Stay on the road until Lobinstown, where you will have clocked up 30km. Continue through Lobinstown, following the sign for Kells. At the junction with the N52, turn left. Cycle to the staggered crossroads at the R162 and cross over to stay on the N52. As a national road, the N52 can be busy and there is no hard shoulder, so proceed with caution.

Continue through Carlanstown towards Kells. On approaching Kells, take the first exit at a roundabout into the town on the R147. At this stage, you will have cycled about 50km. In the centre of town, turn left to pass the Headfort Arms hotel. At the nearby Y-junction, keep left onto the R163 towards Slane. You soon come to the picturesque Headfort Bridge over the River Blackwater and the entrance to Headfort House. Now a school, Headfort House was once home to the 4th Marquis of Headfort and his wife, Rose Boote.

Rose Boote was the daughter of a comedian and a member of the Gaiety Girls, a sensation of the Edwardian London stage. The girls attracted male fans known as 'Stage-door Johnnies'. These men were generally wealthy and aristocratic. Edwardian uproar was caused when Rose married the young and handsome Geoffrey Taylour, 4th Marquis of Headfort. Even King Edward's influence could not deter the couple in love. Though a chorus girl, Rose was well educated and sophisticated. Eventually, Edwardian society accepted the couple after Rose's appearance at a snobby VIP event. The society papers reported her 'bearing herself in a manner which everyone declared to be perfect'. Though the marriage was not predicted to last, it did. She died in 1958 at the age of eighty, outliving her husband by fifteen years.

Continue towards Slane, keeping to the R163, and pass a sign for Telltown Earthworks. This is an ancient Celtic site like Tara. Continue to the staggered crossroads at Kilberry. Turn right and then immediately left by the thatched pub towards Slane, keeping to the R163. Continue cycling to a T-junction and turn right. Soon after, you arrive at another junction at the entrance to Slane Castle. If you need a break, it has a bar and distillery and you can take a tour in season. Turn left, while facing the Castle entrance, to the signalled crossroads in the centre of Slane. For the more energetic, divert left onto the N2 to climb the famous Hill of Slane. Look out for the sign indicating the left turn to the Hill. The round trip is about 3km.

Though St Patrick is regarded as more Irish than the Irish themselves, he came from Roman Britain to convert the pagan Irish to Christianity. This he did with great imagination, such as comparing the three leaves of the shamrock to the Holy Trinity. Another one of his initiatives was at Slane. As the Celtic druids prepared to celebrate the spring equinox on the Hill of Tara, Patrick prepared for the Christian Easter celebration on the Hill of Slane. He lit his fire before the druids lit theirs. As the flames lit up the Slane sky, the druids warned the High King Laegaire that if Patrick's fire was not extinguished, it would burn forever in Ireland. The pagan prophecy proved to be true, so far anyway, though a little wobbly in recent times.

If you decide not to cycle the Hill of Slane, turn right at the traffic lights onto the N2 and cycle down the hill to cross over the River Boyne. Start climbing the hill on the other side and take the first left-hand turn at a

Scanlon's pub at Kilberry.

45

Slane Castle

crossroads. Continue, with the Boyne below on the left, to a T-junction. Turn left, following the brown sign for the Boyne Valley Drive. At the next junction nearby, follow the road left towards Donore. Pass the entrance to the site of Newgrange passage tomb and continue through Donore

An old water pump at Kilberry

village towards Drogheda. At each of two roundabouts, take the second exit to cross over the M1. Cycle to another roundabout, taking the second exit again, towards Drogheda town centre. Continue straight on until you come to traffic lights at a T-junction. The bus station is on the left. Turn right here and continue to the traffic lights at the railway station entrance, before an overhead railway bridge. Turn left at the lights to the station.

7. Drogheda-to-Monasterboice Loop

Drogheda – Tullyallen – Mellifont – Monasterboice – Drogheda

Distance (km): 32	**Score:** ✶ ✶ ✶ ✶
Cycling Time (hours): 1½ to 2	**Traffic:** 2
Grade: 2	**Train Station:** Drogheda MacBride
Gain: 312m	**Grid Reference:** O 098 748

Take a cycle back in time to the land of saints and scholars. Monasterboice and Mellifont represent two monastic periods in Irish history, both different. This relatively easy route offers some pleasant views from the few hills.

River Boyne at Oldbridge, County Meath.

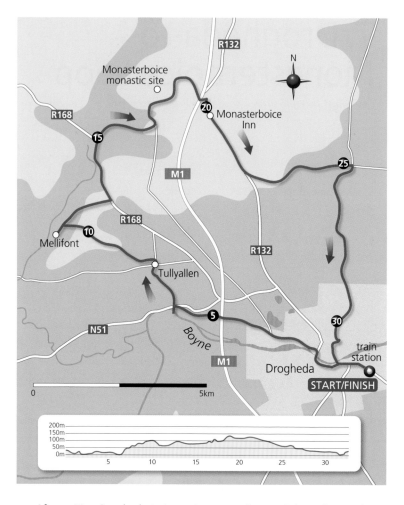

After exiting Drogheda train station car park, turn right at the nearby traffic lights towards the town centre. Continue straight on to the dual carriageway that eventually veers right over the River Boyne. After crossing the river, turn left in the direction of Navan. Having cycled about 3km from the railway station, you will find a left-hand turn opposite an Aldi shop. Take this left, following a sign for Local Traffic. Cycle on until you reach a T-junction with the N51. Turn left towards Navan. Continue to a crossroads where you turn right for Tullyallen onto the L2321, also called King William's Glen. Climb the hill to a crossroads on the outskirts of Tullyallen.

In late June 1690, King William III's army set up camp on the high ground behind the village of Tullyallen. Opposite him, on the south side of the River Boyne, was his nemesis King James II and his Jacobite army. William's encampment of 36,000 men, accompanying baggage, stores, hospital, camp followers, wagons and thousands of horses would have occupied a large area at the expense of locals. On the eve of the battle, William was on reconnaissance near the river. A round fired from a Jacobite cannon hit him on the shoulder. Jacobite celebrations were premature as William suffered only a mild flesh wound and was soon riding triumphantly amongst his troops. Today, it's hard to imagine peaceful Tullyallen as a bustling army campsite preparing for battle.

Go through the crossroads at Tullyallen and soon after, take the left turn. The road rises and eventually pleasant views of the Louth countryside appear on the left, though the cement works at Platin some 8km away dominate. The road then descends to a crossroads where you turn left to Mellifont Abbey.

In 1142, the first Cistercians came to Ireland at the invitation of St Malachy, Archbishop of Armagh. He felt the Irish had strayed from Rome because the Vikings had encouraged, albeit rather forcibly, their pagan values from the ninth century. The saint had visited the famous Cistercian monastery of Clairvaux on his way to Rome. He was impressed and asked St Bernard,

The early thirteenth-century lavabo at Old Mellifont Abbey, the first Cistercian abbey in Ireland.

the abbot there, to train some of his Irish monks on the Cistercian way of life. These monks, together with about ten French counterparts, founded Mellifont Abbey. However, all was not rosy in the chapter house. The French became frustrated with the Irish, who were somewhat lax in adhering to the strict Cistercian rules. In particular, the Irish wouldn't stop talking, in spite of their vow of silence. Anyway, the French monks took the sulks and went home, which gave the Irish plenty to talk about.

On leaving Mellifont, cycle straight ahead until you reach the R168. Turn left onto it, following the sign for Monasterboice, 7km away. Continue to a Y-junction and veer right onto the L2299, signposted for Monasterboice. Soon after, take the left turn to continue to the old monastic settlement. On approach, the tall round tower of Monasterboice with the conical top missing dominates. Founded by St Buithe in the sixth century, the monastic site is famous for its sculpted Celtic crosses.

After a thousand years, the amazing sculptures on Muirdeach's Cross are still clear, a great tribute to the craftspeople back then. On the eastern side of the cross is a very creative depiction of St Michael weighing a human

The tenth-century South Cross and round tower at Monasterboice.

soul on the scales of judgement. Too much sinful weight and the soul becomes eternal turf for Satan's fire. To make sure things go his way, Satan is lying under the opposite end of the scales, pulling down to influence the weigh-in. Meanwhile, Michael is trying to clout the devil with his staff. I can only imagine the conversation between the two. 'No cheating!' says Michael, as he gives Satan a dig. Satan smirks, 'Who do you think invented cheating?' and pulls all the harder.

Continue on from the old monastic site to a T-junction. Turn right onto the L6292 towards the village of Monasterboice. Cycle to a roundabout and take the second exit following the sign for Dunleer and the R132. Cross under the M1 motorway to a T-junction and turn right onto the R132 towards Drogheda. Pass the Monasterboice Inn on the left. Soon after you begin a descent. Look out for the left-hand turn signposted for Termonfeckin on the Cockle road and take it. After taking the turn, there is a grand view to the right over Drogheda. Continue to a crossroads and turn right. Though it is not signposted, this road will lead to Drogheda. After cycling about 27km from the start, you pass Listoke Gardens on the left.

Continue past Listoke to a mini-roundabout near Lourdes Church in Drogheda and take the first exit. Follow the road as it eventually veers

left on a one-way system. Take the following two right-hand turns and pass the nearby school near the old steeple known as the Magdalene Tower. The road then veers to the left and finally ends at the pedestrianised crossroads in the centre of Drogheda. Go through the crossroads and cross St Mary's Bridge over the Boyne. Then take the second left onto the Dublin road and continue past the service station to the railway station traffic lights, just before the overhead bridge. Turn left for the train station.

The fourteenth-century Magdalene Tower, Drogheda, a remnant of a Dominican friary founded in 1224.

8. Drogheda-to-Slane Loop

Drogheda – Newgrange – Slane – Donore – Drogheda

Distance (km): 44	**Score:** ✱ ✱ ✱ ✱
Cycling Time (hours): 2–2½	**Traffic:** 2
Grade: 2	**Train Station:** Drogheda MacBride
Gain: 322m	**Grid Reference:** O 098 748

This route is brimming with myth, history and heritage in the enchanting Boyne Valley, a gem in Ireland's Ancient East. Two major drivers of Ireland's future course transpired here, the Stone Age passage tombs of Brú na Bóinne and the Battle of the Boyne in 1690.

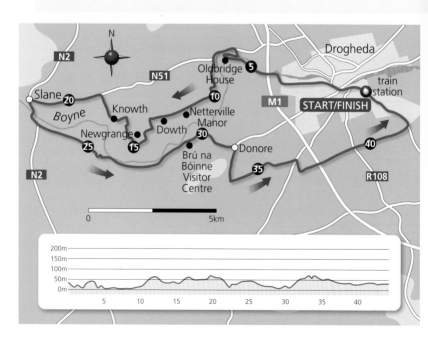

Exit Drogheda train station car park and at the nearby traffic lights, turn right towards the town centre. Continue straight on, passing St Mary's Church on the left, until reaching the traffic lights at McDonald's restaurant on the right. There is a choice of cycling the 'ramparts' in dry weather or taking the road in wet weather. To choose the 'ramparts', cross to McDonald's and pass it and the petrol station to a track that descends to the riverbank. Follow the track west along the River Boyne and then onto a boardwalk near the Mary McAleese motorway bridge. This pedestrian/cycle way is called the Boyneside Trail. It terminates at the entrance to the Battle of the Boyne Visitor Centre, 6km from the railway station.

The alternative (see map) is to take the road. Follow the road past McDonald's until it veers right to cross over the river. At this point, continue straight onto the Rathmullen road and avoid crossing the river. Climb a hill and pass through a signalled junction near the top. Descend the hill and at the next T-junction turn right. When the road sweeps left near the Boyne, you can take up the Boyneside Trail on the boardwalk. Follow the trail under the Mary McAleese motorway bridge to the entrance of the Battle of the Boyne visitor centre. Divert to the battle site to see Oldbridge House, a large eighteenth-century country mansion, which houses an exhibition about the battle. There is also a tea pavilion overlooking magnificent walled gardens.

The Battle of the Boyne was fought on 1 July 1690. So why would the Orange tradition celebrate King William's victory over King James on 12 July? One reason is the calendar difference. Ireland employed the Julian calendar in 1690. Then it was ten days behind the Gregorian calendar, which was introduced in 1752 and is still in use today. But adding ten more days leaves the date at 11 July, still one day short. The Orange Order was founded in 1795, over 100 years after the battle. During that time, another day had been added to make up for the inaccuracy of the Julian calendar over the century and this brought the Gregorian calendar date to 12 July. Today, there is a difference of thirteen days.

At the entrance to the Battle of the Boyne site, cross the humpback bridge over the canal. This canal was constructed in the eighteenth century to help navigation of the river. Follow the road, crossing the river itself, to a nearby crossroads. Turn left onto the N51 in the direction of Slane. After passing the entrance to Townley Hall on the right, take the next left-hand turn onto the L1607, signposted for Dowth. The road begins to ascend. Follow it past Netterville Manor where Irish revolutionary, poet and novelist John Boyle O'Reilly was born in 1844. Close by is Dowth, one of the three passage graves of Brú na Bóinne. The grave's mound is about 11km from the railway station. Cycle straight on

The Victorian manor at Netterville, with a twelfth-century tower on the right.

to a T-junction and turn left up a hill to Newgrange, the most famous of the 5,000-year-old passage tombs of Brú na Bóinne. You cannot access Newgrange from here. Access is from the Brú na Bóinne visitor centre which the route will pass later.

The Dagda was a powerful god who owned the land of Brú na Bóinne. His son Aengus considered Newgrange a valuable piece of real estate and set his eye on it. 'Can I have it, Dad?' he asked. 'No way. It's my favourite place,' replied the Dagda. Aengus wasn't to be put off as he saw the potential in the property. He continued to pester his father, whose refusals were equally adamant. However, Aengus sensed his father was weakening and, thinking quickly, he asked, 'Will you let me stay the day and night?' His father sighed but agreed, to get his son out of his hair. The following day the Dagda checked the passage tomb, expecting his son to have vacated the premises. But he was still there. 'I thought we agreed one day and night,' he said. Aengus smiled. 'We didn't agree one day and night. We agreed day and night.'

Cycle past Newgrange and nearby Newgrange farm. The road narrows to a little-used boreen with grass running along the middle. Enjoy the views from here. The boreen eventually descends to a T-junction. Turn left and cycle past Knowth, the third passage tomb of Brú na Bóinne. Knowth is world-famous for its megalithic art. Continue following the road to a T-junction with the N51. Turn left towards Slane onto this narrow busy road for 3km. Pass by the cottage museum to the poet Francis Ledwidge and continue into Slane, about 20km from the start. At the traffic lights, turn left onto the N2. Descend a steep hill and cross the narrow bridge over the River Boyne, then begin a climb on the other side. Take the first turn left onto the L16002. The road follows the Boyne before the river veers away and the road eventually terminates at a T-junction. Turn left and cycle to another T-junction. Turn left again

Newgrange passage tomb, built c. 3350 BC.

in the direction of Donore, 7km away. The Boyne will appear again on the left.

Aengus's mother, Boann, bore her son after she had an affair with the Dagda. Boann is said to have created the River Boyne. Legend tells of an enchanted well called the Well of Segais. Nine hazel trees of great wisdom

Passage tombs at Knowth.

surrounded it. Hazelnuts fell from the trees into the well and filled its waters with knowledge. Only Nechtan, keeper of the Well, and his cupbearers could approach it. Stubborn Boann defied the rule and challenged the power of Segais by walking widdershins, or anticlockwise, around it. In anger, Segais's waters burst forth and surged to the sea like a great serpent to create the River Boyne. Boann was seized by the waters and carried to her death, probably dashed by the wise but angry hazelnuts.

At 28km from the start, pass the entrance to Brú na Bóinne Visitor Centre, where there is a coffee shop. Continue to a T-junction in Donore village. Turn right, following the sign for Duleek. Take the next left turn at about 33km from the start and continue to a T-junction. Keep right here and pass the Platin Cement works to a crossroads. Cycle straight across and continue to a second crossroads nearby. Turn left and continue straight on until you come to a roundabout. Take the first exit to the next roundabout and again take the first exit. Continue towards Drogheda town centre. After passing under a railway bridge, turn right at the next traffic lights to the railway station.

Medieval Slane Abbey on the Hill of Slane.

9. Dundalk-to-Annagassan Loop

Dundalk – Louth village – Castlebellingham – Annagassan – Dundalk

Distance (km): 76		**Score:** ✳ ✳ ✳	
Cycling Time (hours): 3¾–4¼		**Traffic:** 2	
Grade: 2		**Train Station:** Dundalk Clarke	
Gain: 322m		**Grid Reference:** J 041 069	

This is a relatively flat route to tour the sleepy villages and picturesque coast of Louth. Annagassan was a great Viking port from which the Norsemen pillaged monasteries near and far. Louth village was a location of a monastic settlement and the remains are still there today.

Clochafarmore near Knockbridge, County Louth.

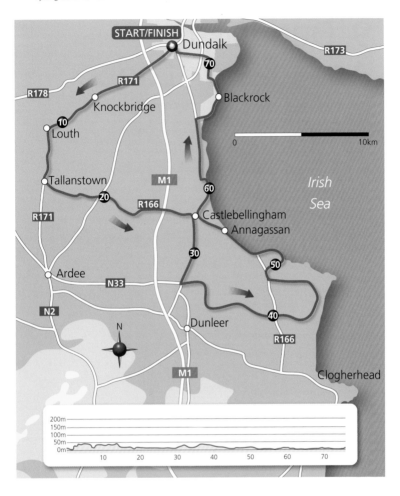

On exiting Dundalk train station car park, turn left. At the nearby roundabout, take the second exit onto the R171 towards Knockbridge. After 2km, keep right to stay on the R171. Having cycled 4km from Dundalk, look out for the small information board about Clochafarmore. This standing stone is in a field on the left after the turn for the L31671, also on the left.

If you've been to the GPO in Dublin you'll have seen a bronze statue by Oliver Sheppard. It depicts the legendary Ulster warrior Cúchulainn tied to a stone with a raven perched on his shoulder. The stone of Clochafarmore ('stone of the big man') is that stone. Legend says that Cúchulainn, while defending Ulster against Queen Maeve of Connacht, was fatally wounded at this place. He tied himself to the stone to face her army. Maeve's soldiers dared not approach, such was their fear of the great warrior. Finally, the Morrigan, the Celtic goddess of War and Death, appeared in the form of a raven and landed on his shoulder. It was only then that Maeve's soldiers celebrated the end of the big man.

Continue to the flower-lined village of Knockbridge. As you enter, note St Mary's Church on the right. It's worth checking out the three Harry Clarke stained-glass windows over the altars. Cycle straight through Knockbridge to Louth village, about 12km from Dundalk. In the centre of Louth, divert right to see the ruins of fourteenth-century St Mary's Abbey and St Mochta's House. St Mochta was a disciple of St Patrick, though his house was built after his death.

Louth is named after Lugh, a great god of the Celts. He was known for his skills in arts and crafts, amongst many others. He once arrived to a party at the great hall at Tara, hosted by the high king of Ireland. The guard at the door insisted that only one person with a particular skill could enter. Lugh lists in turn all the skills he has and each time the guard responds with, 'Sorry, but we've already got somebody who can do that.' Exasperated, Lugh scratched his head before finally asking, 'Ah, but do you have somebody who can do them all?' Lugh was allowed in.

Cycle straight through Louth towards Tallanstown on the R171. At about 15km from Dundalk, arrive at a T-junction and turn right. On entering Tallanstown, take the left turn onto the R166 towards Castlebellingham. Continue following the R166 to a T-junction with the R132 at Castlebellingham. Turn right onto the R132, signposted for Dunleer. While cycling through the town, pass the castellated entrance to Bellingham Castle on the right. Bellingham Castle is now a hotel.

St Mochta's House, Louth village.

Bellingham Castle, Castlebellingham.

Castlebellingham gets its name from the Bellingham family, who owned lands here from the seventeenth century and built Bellingham Castle. One Colonel Thomas Bellingham was guide to King William III at the Battle of the Boyne. A great man for describing each day's weather in his diary, he says it was 'excessive hott' on 1 July 1690, the day of the battle. After a busy day defeating the Jacobite army, he left King William at Duleek where the king spent the night. The colonel himself returned to the site of battle at Oldbridge. On his return he wrote, 'I was almost fainte from want of drink and meat.' I'm sure he made short work of both.

Continue on the R132 to a staggered crossroads, about 32km from the start. Turn left, following the sign for Drumcar. Cycle on to a T-junction and turn right. Follow the road to the next T-junction and this time turn left. At about 38km, cycle through a crossroads. After passing an old cemetery, there is another crossroads. Cycle through, following the sign for Dunany. At the next T-junction, turn left and left again at the following staggered crossroads. The coast comes into view. Continue on this road to the junction with R166, passing an old church on the way. Turn right onto the R166 towards Annagassan. About 1km further, turn right again off the R166 towards the coast. Keep right after passing a thatched cottage, following the sign for Scenic Route. Arriving at the water's edge, the views of the Cooley and Mourne mountains are stunning. At about the 53km mark, the road rejoins the R166. Turn right towards nearby Annagassan.

Annagassan, or Linn Duchaill, is the site of an important longphort, a Viking encampment used as a base for raiding. First mentioned in the Annals in

AD 841, the year Dublin was founded, for a time it rivalled the future capital in importance. In 842 the Annagassan Vikings plundered Clonmacnoise and captured the abbot of Clogher. In 852 they destroyed Armagh. As time passed, the Irish got the upper hand and expelled them in 891. The Viking hordes returned but by 927 the longphort was no more.

Cycle through the village and cross the old bridge over the River Dee. Continue on the R166 towards Castlebellingham. As you enter Castlebellingham, there is a sharp bend going to the left. Carefully, take the L6188 off this bend to the right. The road leads back to the coast to an area known as Seabank, a good spot for watching lapwing, golden plover and black-tailed godwit. The road eventually swings away from the coast to a junction with the R132. Turn right towards Dundalk.

At about 65km from the start, take the right turn onto the R172 towards Blackrock. At Blackrock, enjoy the seafront views as you cycle through. The road eventually turns away from the coast, passing the Loakers Wetlands, teeming with birdlife. Views of the Cooley Mountains dominate the scene. Eventually, the road comes to a roundabout. Take the first exit, following the R172 and sign for the town centre. At the next roundabout, take the second exit, staying on the R172. The road finally terminates at traffic lights at the R132. Turn right, followed by a left towards Knockbridge. Follow the road around to the right to a roundabout. Take the first exit and continue past the nearby Great Northern Distillery. The right-hand turn for the railway station is after the distillery.

The seafront at Blackrock, County Louth.

10. Dundalk-to-Ardee Loop

Dundalk – Tallanstown – Ardee – Dromiskin – Dundalk

Distance (km): 64	**Score:** ✳ ✳ ✳ ✳
Cycling Time (hours): 3–3½	**Traffic:** 2
Grade: 2	**Train Station:** Dundalk Clarke
Gain: 307m	**Grid Reference:** J 041 069

There are no hilly challenges on this route as it passes through the lovely Louth countryside. It is dotted with pretty villages that are a tribute to their local communities.

Great Northern Distillery, Dundalk, County Louth.

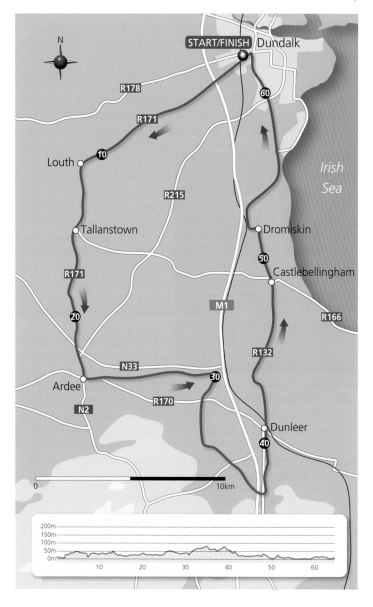

On leaving Dundalk train station car park, turn left and note the Great Northern Brewery next to the station.

Since the late 1600s brewing has been an important part of Dundalk business. In 1896, the Great Northern Brewery was established on this site. It later became the home of Harp Lager where that brew was produced for about fifty years. Harp production moved to Dublin in 2013 and the plant changed from brewery to distillery, producing single malt, pot still and single grain whiskey. Dundalk is well suited to distilling because of the availability of pure water from the nearby Cooley Mountains. Now, isn't that a sound reason for drinking Dundalk whiskey?

One of the Harry Clarke stained-glass windows at St Mary's Church, Knockbridge.

Cycle past the Great Northern Brewery to the nearby round-about and take the second exit onto the R171 towards Knockbridge. After 2km, keep right to stay on the R171. Continue to the village of Knockbridge. As you enter, note St Mary's Church on the right in which there are three Harry Clarke stained-glass windows over the altars. Cycle straight through Knockbridge to the village of Louth, about 12km from Dundalk. In the centre of Louth, divert right to see the ruins of St Mary's Abbey and St Mochta's House or continue straight through towards Tallanstown on the R171. After cycling 15km from Dundalk, arrive at a T-junction and turn right to nearby Tallanstown. At the crossroads in the centre of the tidy village, is a sculpture of Vere Foster under the shade of a whitebeam tree.

Philanthropist, educationalist and genuine Irishman, though born in Amsterdam, Vere Foster was a regular visitor to his brother at Glyde House near Tallanstown. Like his father, Foster worked in the foreign service but, shocked by the plight of Irish famine victims, he gave up his job to help. He went on to finance emigration for many victims, especially women. Having experienced the terrible conditions on the so-called 'coffin ships', he lobbied parliament to force the shipping companies improve passenger conditions. His vision of education as a way out of poverty led him to finance the construction of national schools, Tallanstown being the first. Foster was the first president of the Irish National Teachers Organisation (INTO) and developed the Vere Foster's Writing Copy-Books for schools.

Having spent most of his finances on projects for the poor, he died in frugal lodgings in 1900.

At the crossroads in Tallanstown, turn left, staying on the R171 towards Ardee. Outside the village, pass the striking neo-Gothic entrance to the old graveyard. Continue to Ardee. As you enter the town, take the second exit off the Carrickmacross roundabout. At the following mini-roundabout, take the second exit into Ardee town centre.

During the Jacobite/Williamite War of 1689–91, Ardee was ravaged as the warring armies passed through like a plague of locusts, stripping the area to supply a moving mass of 60,000 men, thousands of horses and equipment. The Rev. George Walker, a Williamite, described the results on the local people. 'There were none of the Irish to be seen, but a few starved creatures who had scraped up some of the Husks of Oats nigh a mill to eat instead of better food. It's a wonder to see how some of those creatures live; I myself have seen them scratching like hens amongst the cinders for victuals.'

Cycle through the town, passing Ardee Castle, to the old bridge over the River Dee. On the right, before crossing the bridge, is a sculpture of Cuchulainn holding his foster brother Ferdia after slaying him in battle. Cross the bridge and take the next left turn onto the R170 towards Dunleer. On the edge of Ardee, cycle straight onto a local road, leaving the R170, which veers right. Continue to the end of this road and then turn right towards Dromin. At a three-way junction, take the rightmost road and cycle on to a crossroads. Go across onto the L2254, signposted for Tinure, to the next crossroads. Go straight again. Eventually, arrive at

Ardee Castle, built in the fifteenth century, is the largest fortified medieval tower house in the country.

a staggered junction at the R132 about 38km from the start. Turn left for Dunleer.

There was a story told hereabouts of a farmer whose chickens were being taken by a wily fox. The frustrated farmer decided he had to do something. One night he armed his son with a hatchet and they both sat out of sight, waiting for the fox. Eventually the animal appeared and slunk into the chicken coop. The farmer followed and was soon chasing the fox out of the coop in the direction of his son. The farmer called out, 'Take its head off.' The son looked bewildered and the father called again, 'Take its head off.' The son shrugged and pulled the head off the hatchet. He held it up for his father to see as the fox brushed by.

Cycle through Dunleer towards Castlebellingham, staying on the R132. At about 44km, arrive at a staggered crossroads. Turn right on the R132 towards Castlebellingham; the town is almost 50km from the start. Cycle through Castlebellingham and, after the village green, look out for a thatched café on the left. Turn left at the junction here and then immediately right onto the L7187 for the neat village of Dromiskin. Continue to the crossroads in the centre of the Dromiskin. Divert right to view the old ecclesiastical site linked to St Patrick. Vikings and Irish plundered this site, eventually forcing the monks to leave.

Otherwise, turn left at the crossroads. Follow the road to a T-junction at the R132. Turn left onto the R132 to Dundalk. Continue towards the town centre, passing the wind turbine at the Institute of Technology. Near the town centre, at a set of traffic lights, take the left turn, signposted for Knockbridge and the railway station. Follow the road to a roundabout. Take the first exit towards Carrickmacross, followed by the right turn to the railway station at the Great Northern Brewery.

The road to Dromiskin.

11. Dundalk-to-Castleblaney Loop

Dundalk – Crossmaglen – Castleblaney – Carrickmacross – Inniskeen – Dundalk

Distance (km): 81

Cycling Time (hours): 4–4½

Grade: 3

Gain: 512m

Score: ✳ ✳ ✳

Traffic: 2

Train Station: Dundalk Clarke

Grid Reference: J 041 069

Stretching across the border into Ulster, this route passes through towns and villages touched by artists. There are some hills to contend with; however, lake views help to compensate for the climbing.

Monument in Crossmaglen, County Armagh.

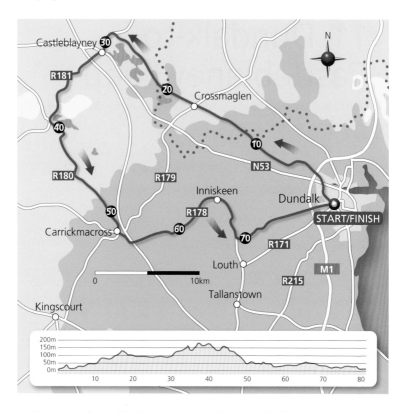

On leaving Dundalk train station car park, turn right, then take the third turn on the right, following the sign for Mount Avenue. Continue to the crossroads at the main Castleblaney road and cycle straight across. About 3km from the station, turn left at a T-junction followed by a left at a sign for Roche GFC. Soon after is a church and cemetery; turn left here. Cycle straight through two crossroads, the second at about 11km from Dundalk. The border into County Armagh is crossed after 12km or thereabouts.

When the border was created, motorists crossing it had to use 'approved' roads controlled by custom posts. The many 'unapproved' roads were patrolled instead to prevent people using them for smuggling. For convenience, motorists from the Republic were permitted to use these unapproved roads while travelling through Northern Ireland, though they couldn't stop or turn off until they re-entered the Republic. These were called 'concession roads'. Apparently, crossing an unapproved road illegally was known as 'jumping the border'. Thankfully, the custom posts are gone

Muckno Lake near Castleblayney, County Monagahan.

and speed-limit signs, indicating the change to miles or kilometres, are the only indication of crossing the border (at least for now).

Continue straight on and after cycling 14km, arrive at a T-junction. Turn right, to leave behind Larkin's Road, followed by a left onto Mong Road. Cycle straight on into Crossmaglen, about 18km from Dundalk.

During 'The Troubles', the old Market House in Crossmaglen was set on fire in 1974 by a unit of the British army stationed in the town. The army claimed there were explosives and arms inside that could not be disposed of safely. So the building was torched. Afterwards, local groups lobbied to have a community centre built and in 1982 permission was granted. Work commenced and the façade of the old market house was combined into the new construction. The centre was officially opened in 1984.

At Cardinal O'Fiaich Square in Crossmaglen, turn right onto Blaney Road. Having cycled 20km, cross the border into County Monaghan. The 80 km/h speed limit signs are the only indications of a return to the Republic. Continue on Blaney Road, passing scenic Muckno Lake on the left, to a T-junction at the R182. Turn left onto the R182, signposted

for Castleblaney. On the outskirts of the town, the road terminates at a T-junction with the R181. Turn left towards the town centre, about 30km from the start.

Continue through the centre of Castleblaney, following the R181 towards Shercock. The R181 is a bit of a rollercoaster from here. It has more humps than a string of camels. Eventually, arrive at a junction with the R180 near Lough Egish. Turn left onto the R180 and continue to Carrickmacross, about 14km away. On the outskirts of the town, turn right at the T-junction stop sign. In the centre of Carrickmacross, turn left onto the R178 towards Dundalk. Pass St Joseph's Church on the left. It's worth stopping at the church to view the Harry Clarke stained-glass windows inside. Afterwards, divert a short distance on the Crossmaglen Road to the old workhouse cemetery known as Bully's Acre. The cemetery is beside the Primary Care Centre and was the last resting place of a great traditional Irish musician.

At Carrickmacross, County Monaghan.

An ancient tradition died with Patrick Byrne when he was interred in Bully's Acre. Patrick was the last of the great Irish harpers who played professionally for the nobility. Born about 1794, he went to a school for young blind harpers in Belfast. He graduated with sixty tunes and the distinction for acquiring considerable proficiency on the harp. He left for England to entertain the well-to-do there. In Scotland, he played for none other than Queen Victoria and Prince Albert at Balmoral Castle. Returning to Ireland in 1847, he was employed by the Shirley family of Lough Fea estate in Carrickmacross. The great musician died in 1863 and was buried in Bully's Acre, a pauper's cemetery.

Keep right after St Joseph's Church, keeping to the R178 to Inniskeen and Dundalk. As you continue, the River Fane is on the left and is a popular venue for fishing. At the nearby roundabout, take the second exit towards Dundalk and continue to the left turn onto the L4620, the road to Inniskeen. The village is 5km from here. On the far side of the village is the Patrick Kavanagh Resource Centre. It is set in an old church and a simple plot in the surrounding cemetery marks the last resting place of the great poet.

Patrick Kavanagh's poetry represented an Ireland now gone. His poem 'Inniskeen Road: July Evening' harks back to a pre-Lycra-and-helmet cycling generation. The opening lines invoke an image of hopeful young men and women cycling to a dance, no doubt dressed in their Sunday best. The humble bicycle was the main form of transport then, whereas today it's

Metal sculpture of Patrick Kavanagh, Carrickmacross.

an option. Anyway, does anybody cycle to a dance today? They were the good old days, though Kavanagh might not have agreed.

Inniskeen is about 66km from the start. Pass the Patrick Kavanagh Resource Centre and continue to a crossroads at a pub. Turn left onto the R178 towards Dundalk, 10km away. As you continue on this road the Cooley and Mourne mountains dominate the skyline. Eventually, cross over the railway line in Dundalk. Immediately after, turn left into the train station.

Patrick Kavanagh Centre, Inniskeen, County Monaghan.

12. Dundalk-to-Flagstaff Loop

Dundalk – Flagstaff – Omeath – Carlingford – Dundalk

Distance (km): 68	**Score:** ✷ ✷ ✷ ✷
Cycling Time (hours): 3–4	**Traffic:** 2
Grade: 4	**Train Station:** Dundalk Clarke
Gain: 619m	**Grid Reference:** J 041 069

This route takes in the Cooley Peninsula, an area of great natural beauty packed with legend. It is a challenging cycle, rewarded with magnificent scenery and a visit to the popular medieval town of Carlingford.

Dundalk Courthouse, County Louth.

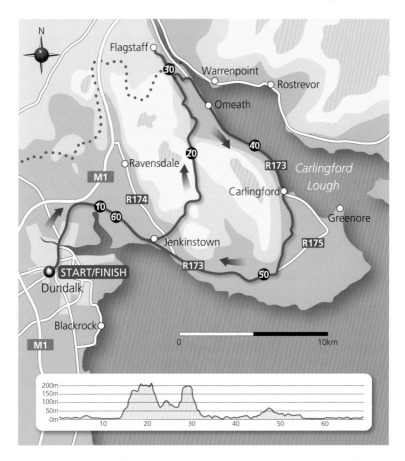

On exiting Dundalk train station car park, turn left. At the nearby roundabout, take the first exit to the town centre. The traffic system changes to one-way. Follow it to the courthouse and take the left turn here onto Clanbrassil Street. Cross over the Castletown River and continue until the end of the road, about 5km from the railway station.

There are two cycle tracks here; take the one on the right, which leads onto the Ballymascanlan roundabout. Take the fourth exit off the roundabout onto the R173 towards Carlingford. After cycling about 13km, turn left onto the L3084, signposted for Omeath. Continue to a staggered crossroads where you turn right and then immediately left, following the signpost for the Táin Trail. The road climbs to the top of a hill and then descends to a water treatment tank on the right. This descent is Jenkinstown's 'magic hill' and is about 15km from the start.

Believe it or not, a bike will freewheel from the water treatment tank up the hill. Try it and then try to freewheel down and see what happens. Magic or what? Needless to say, there are scientific theories like magnetic or gravity effects or, perhaps, it's simply an optical illusion. Actually, it's more likely to be the sleeping Cooley giant, Fionn Mac Cumhaill, inhaling, or the 236 Cooley leprechauns up to shenanigans. By the way, the little fellas are protected by EU directive. Whatever the cause, the effect is magical.

From here, there is a steady climb for 1km. Eventually the road ends at a T-junction; turn left onto the main road. The Long Woman's Grave is nearby on the right.

After his death, the chieftain of Omeath left his lands to his sons Conn Óg and Lorcan. Canny Conn wanted it all, so he took Lorcan to a misty hollow and told him he could have all the land he could see, which wasn't much. Foolish Lorcan fell for it and accepted the misty hollow. After realising he had been duped, he took to the high seas to make his fortune. On a voyage to Spain he met Cauthleen, a well-to-do descendant of the Ulster O'Donnells. He fell in love with the seven-foot beauty. Cauthleen was already engaged

to a wealthy merchant but Lorcan convinced her of his riches in Omeath, telling her he would bring her to a spot in the mountains from where all the land she could see was his. So they eloped and landed at Carlingford. Lorcan took her to his misty hollow. Overwhelmed with disappointment, she

The Long Woman's Grave on the Cooley Peninsula.

collapsed on the spot and died. Lorcan, realising his deceit had backfired, flung himself into a deep bog nearby. Cauthleen was buried at the site, now known as the Long Woman's grave. She sleeps in eternal disappointment while he wallows heartbroken in the murky bog.

Pass the Long Woman's Grave. At the next junction, turn right in the direction of Omeath and soon Carlingford Lough and the Mourne Mountains come into view. Descend the hill to the outskirts of Omeath and to a school on the left. Take the first left turn after the school. Cycle up a hill to a T-junction and turn right. Follow the road to a crossroads and turn left at the signpost for Jonesborough. From here, there is a stiff climb over the border to the viewing point at the Flagstaff, about 28km from Dundalk.

The views from the Flagstaff are stunning. Fjord or not, Carlingford Lough is a scene to behold, sandwiched between the Mourne and Cooley Mountains. Below, where the lough starts to narrow, is Omeath and on the opposite side Warrenpoint. Look towards the sea: Greenore can be seen in the distance; Slieve Gullion dominates the inland view.

On leaving the Flagstaff, cycle back to the crossroads and continue straight through. Follow the road to the T-junction at the R173. Turn right onto the R173 to Omeath by the shore of Carlingford Lough. Cycle through the village towards Carlingford. Outside Omeath, there is the option to take the 6km greenway; look out for the signposts. This is a stony track for very leisurely cyclists and pedestrians. It terminates at the marina near Carlingford.

Whether taking the greenway or the road, eventually pass King John's Castle on the left overlooking Carlingford Harbour.

Perched on a rocky footing, St John's Castle commands a strong position and fine views over Carlingford Lough and the town. Sandwiched between Slieve Foye and the Mourne Mountains, the setting is quite magnificent. Most likely built by Hugh de Lacy, its survival is a mark of the longevity of Norman construction. The original castle consisted of an enclosed D-shaped courtyard with two rectangular towers at the entrance. The eastern section was built later and included a great hall. St John's Castle got its name from a reputed visit by King John in 1210 when he came to Ireland to control his nemesis Walter de Lacy (of Trim Castle). There is now a plan and funds available to refurbish the castle back to its glory days. At the time of writing, the castle was not open to the public.

Carlingford Lough viewed from the Flagstaff, with the Mourne Mountains on the left and Slieve Foye on the right.

St Patrick's Church, Dundalk.

After the castle, take the right turn signposted for the town centre. At the nearby T-junction turn left and immediately right into the centre. Follow the road to the left away from the town centre towards Dundalk. This is the R173. At the Y-junction just after the church, keep right to stay on the R173.

Eventually the R173 comes to a T-junction with the main Dundalk-to-Carlingford and Greenore road. This was the site of Bush railway station; part of the Dundalk-to-Greenore line opened in 1873 and closed in 1951. There is also a sculpture of the Brown Bull of Cooley over which Queen Maeve of Connacht declared war on Ulster. Turn right onto the main road in the direction of Dundalk. At this stage, the distance cycled is 48km.

Continue to the Ballymascanlan roundabout. Pass the first exit and look out for the cycle track originally taken from Dundalk. Follow it to the road and continue to the bridge over the Castletown River. After crossing the bridge, turn left to follow the one-way system. Continue into town and at the courthouse turn left and then right, passing nineteenth-century St Patrick's Church, a fine Gothic-style building built of Newry granite. Follow the road straight on until the right-hand turn signposted for Knockbridge. Turn right here and cycle to the roundabout. Take the second exit towards the railway station. It's just after the Great Northern Brewery on the right.

13. Laytown-to-Navan Loop

Laytown – Duleek – Navan – Donore – Laytown

Distance (km): 75
Cycling Time (hours): 3½–4
Grade: 2
Gain: 308m

Score: ✴ ✴ ✴ ✴
Traffic: 2
Train Station: Laytown
Grid Reference: O 162 713

A very pleasant route with stretches to put the head down and push the legs. There are some lovely views, with an exceptional one at Ardmulchan Church and all without much hill climbing.

Lime tree at Duleek, County Meath.

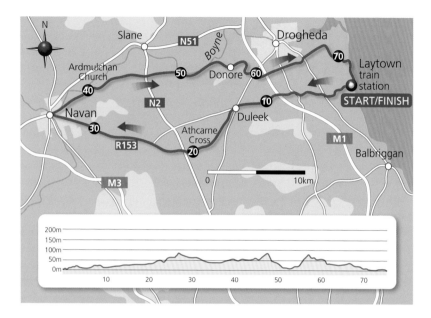

On exiting Laytown train station, cross the road towards the car park and then cross the pedestrian bridge over the River Nanny. Turn right on the other side and cycle under the green railway bridge. Follow the road for about 1.5km to the first right-hand turn. Take this turn and continue to the T-junction at a school. Turn right towards the centre of Julianstown and descend the hill. Take the left-hand turn onto the L56221, just before crossing the bridge. At the end of L56221, turn right and then left onto the R150 towards Duleek. Continue cycling to a T-junction on the outskirts of Duleek. Note the path on the opposite side of the road and cross to it. Follow the path to the road leading into Duleek and cycle into the village.

In a grassy square in the village there are a number of trees. One is a lime planted on a mound and higher than the others. In the late seventeenth century, two saplings, a lime and an ash, were planted here to represent King William III and his wife, Queen Mary. The story begins when their uncle, King Charles II, arranged the couple's marriage for political reasons. The romance got off to a rocky start. On Mary's first sight of William, the fifteen-year old thought her life was at an end. At twenty-seven, her groom and first cousin was small, hunched and sported a large hooked nose. The wedding was a gloomy occasion. The bride cried and the groom was uneasy. The only one who seemed pleased was Charles, who smiled and joked in an attempt to lighten the mood.

Surprisingly, the marriage proved successful. William and Mary were crowned joint monarchs of England, Ireland and Scotland, having first deposed Mary's father, James II, who had succeeded Charles II. Alas, the loving couple did not live happily ever after. In 1694, Mary caught smallpox. William was distraught and kept a vigil at her bedside till her death. More tragedy followed when, in 1702, William's horse stumbled. William was gravely injured and died soon after. Next to his heart, a lock of Mary's hair and her wedding ring were found. With regard to the lime and ash trees, the ash is gone but the lime still stands on the mound. The ash left a mark on the lime just as Mary did on William. The indent is on the northern side of the trunk towards the site of the Battle of the Boyne, where William defeated Mary's father in 1690.

Continue through the centre of Duleek to a nearby Y-junction, about 14km from Laytown. Turn left here onto the L1610, signposted for Trim. Eventually, pass the Athcarne wayside cross on the right. It was erected to the memory of Sir Luke Bathe around 1675. The ruins of his Tudor-style castle can be found down the left-hand turn just before the cross. Continue to the N2. Turn right and immediately left towards Navan on the R153. Continue through Kentstown and cycle on to Navan, sticking to the R153. Near the town centre, there is a right-hand turn signposted for Beauparc and the Táin Trail on the L3400. The option for a break is to continue over the nearby bridge into the town centre and return to the L3400 later. Navan is about 34km from Drogheda.

Athcarne Cross near Duleek.

The Times of 4 October 1898 reported a fatal biting incident on the Navan-to-Dublin train. A thirty-year-old woman and her husband were found by the ticket collector to be drunk. He moved the drunken pair to a carriage with four or five others sharing the same condition. During the journey a row broke out and the woman was bitten in the forefinger of her right hand by one of the men. Unfortunately, she died later. At the coroner's inquest, medical evidence proved her death was due to congestion of the lungs and heart failure arising from tetanus. The bite was the culprit. The coroner's jury found a verdict in accordance with the testimony and condemned the practice of railway companies of allowing drunken persons to travel on trains.

Take the L3400, which is part of the Boyne Valley Drive. At about 39km from the start, there is a left-hand turn for Ardmulchan Church. It's well worth diverting the short distance for the view over the River Boyne and Dunmoe Castle. Otherwise, continue to the staggered crossroads at the N2 and cross to the L1600, staying on the Boyne Valley Drive. The road ascends to provide fine views over the Meath countryside from both sides of the road. After cycling 50km, the white quartz of the Newgrange mound comes into view on the other side of the River Boyne. Pass by Brú na Bóinne visitor centre, entry to the passage tombs of Newgrange and Knowth. Continue into Donore village, about 55km from the start.

Follow the road out of Donore. After passing the Roadstone Mullaghcrone entrance, take the next right turn. Platin Cement works will dominate in front of you. Continue on, eventually passing the cement works, to a crossroads. Continue straight across and at the next crossroads turn left. Cycle on, crossing over the M1, to a roundabout

The Bull of Navan, created by Galway sculptor Colin Grehan in 2011.

about 65km from the start. Take the first exit to a second roundabout and here take the second exit in the direction of Mornington on the L1611. Continue to the centre of Donacarney and turn right onto the R150 towards Bettystown and Laytown. Cycle on to a roundabout at Wheatfield and take the second exit (the first is not in use). At the next roundabout, take the first exit into the centre of Bettystown.

River Boyne at Ardmulchan Church near Navan.

The magnificent ninth-century Tara Brooch was found at Bettystown in 1850. The children of a poor local woman came across it near the beach. She brought it to an ironmonger in Drogheda who, thinking it was junk, sent her away. However, undeterred, she brought it to a watchmaker who gave her a few pence for it. The watchmaker cleaned it up and took it to Waterhouse & Co., a Dublin jeweller. He sold it for about the same number of pounds as he gave the poor woman in pence. Waterhouse gave it the fancy title of Tara even though it has nothing to do with Tara. Apparently, Celtic revivalism was popular amongst the middle class then and Waterhouse saw this as a business opportunity. The brooch, crafted at the peak of early medieval Irish metalworking, now rests in the National Museum, away from the salty sands of Bettystown.

At the T-junction in the centre of Bettystown, turn right towards Laytown on the R150. Continue into Laytown and follow the road until it veers to the right away from the coast. Nearby is a car park and the railway station is opposite.

14. Longford-to-Ballymahon Figure of Eight

Longford – Ballymahon – Keenagh – Ardagh – Longford

Distance (km): 56	Score: ✳ ✳ ✳
Cycling Time (hours): 2½–3¼	Traffic: 2
Grade: 3	Train Station: Longford
Gain: 278m	Grid Reference: N 134 749

Heritage and literature feature on this route with hills that require little work. I cycled this on a clear, sunny autumn morning that showcased the green and gold of the lovely Longford countryside.

Statue of Oliver Goldsmith at Ballymahon, County Longford.

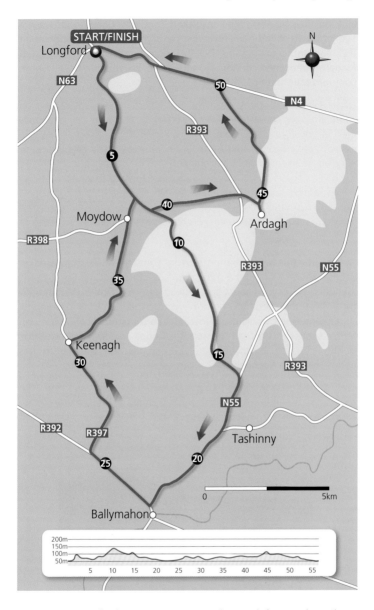

On exiting Longford train station car park, turn left over the railway bridge and follow the road as it veers to the right nearby. After cycling about 1km, turn left and soon there is a signpost for Keenagh and Moydow pointing the way. About 7km from Longford, there is a Y-junction. Keep left here, following the sign for Ardagh. Continue on this road until reaching the N55. Turn right onto the N55, signposted for Ballymahon, and continue into the town. Ballymahon is 23km from Longford train station.

Oliver Goldsmith, poet, novelist and jack-of-many-trades, lived in Ballymahon for about three years. A bit of an eccentric, he sometimes lived in poverty but managed to remain charitable. A story is told of a woman who asked him for help to feed her hungry family. Responding to her pleas, he went to his frugal lodgings, took his blanket and coverlet off the bed and gave them to the woman to sell for food. The next morning, a friend called, only to see the bare feather mattress on the bed but no sign of Goldsmith. The friend called out and to his surprise a face popped through a slit in the mattress. In order to beat the chill, Goldsmith had slept between the feathers.

At the T-junction in Ballymahon, turn right onto the R392 signposted for Lanesborough. Continue out the road and cross over the Royal Canal, identified by bicycles and a flower-filled boat. At 26km turn right onto the R397, signposted for Longford and Keenagh. Continue to Keenagh.
   On entering the village, detour left at a car park following the sign for Lanesborough, to visit the Iron Age Corlea Trackway visitor centre. Continue on and take the left turn at the sign for the visitor centre. It is about 3km from Keenagh.

The Corlea Trackway is an Iron Age bog road dating back to 148 BC. The oak road is the largest of its kind found in Europe and an 18-metre section is on display in the visitor centre in a room designed to preserve this

Outside Ballymahon near the canal-side track.

Route 14: Longford-to-Ballymahon Figure of Eight

ancient wonder. The road was constructed to allow the wheeled vehicles of the time to pass over the bog. However, it is believed the road soon sank into the peat where it remained until discovered in 1984. The surrounding bog itself has been protected to ensure the buried section is preserved. Opening times are seasonal and checking with the visitor centre is advised

In the centre of Keenagh village there is a clock tower erected to Lawrence Harman King-Harman. Turn right at the clock tower, following the sign for Moydow and Cycling Route 2A. At the next junction, leave the cycling route by continuing straight on towards Moydow. Having cycled 33km, veer left at a Y-junction to stay on the main road. Pass the ancient Augustinian monastery of Abbeyderg and continue to a junction at a pub. Stay on the main road by veering left following the sign for Moydow. Pass by a ruined church and old cemetery at Moydow.

A family called Jessop were landowners in Moydow. They are said to have got the estate in a less-than-scrupulous way. After Cromwell's campaign in Ireland, one of his soldiers came to Longford to take possession of lands granted to him for his military service. A wily Longford butler agreed to show the soldier his new property. Taking him to the top of nearby Castlerea Mountain on a blustery wet day, he pointed to the bleakest and most infertile part of the soldier's new property. The soldier wasn't impressed and said if he got £5 and a horse he would sell the lot. The

butler had no hesitation in taking up the offer. The soldier rode off with a fiver in his pocket and the Jessop era began. However, the past came knocking when the last Jessop gambled the estate on a game of cards and managed to lose the lot. Easy come, easy go!

After the ruined church and old cemetery, arrive at a T-junction by a modern cemetery and turn right, following the signpost for Ardagh. Continue to the first left-hand turn and take it. Although there are signposts here, none indicate the direction of this left turn. Having cycled a total of 43km, arrive at a crossroads at the R393 and go straight across. At the nearby T-junction, turn right into the heritage town of Ardagh.

The Gothic Revival clock tower at Keenagh, designed in 1878 and still in working order.

85

Not only a significant centre of religious and architectural history, Ardagh is also associated with literature. The village features incognito in Oliver Goldsmith's comedy *She Stoops to Conquer*. Based on his own experience of mistaken identity, Goldsmith went to Ardagh House after a local fooled him into believing it was an inn. The house was the home of a landed gentry family called Fetherstone. Having enjoyed their food and drink, the brash young Goldsmith proceeded to court Miss Fetherstone, thinking she was a servant. His embarrassment later turned to humour when he made use of the experience for his comedy play.

Church ruins and cemetery, Moydow.

On leaving Ardagh, retrace the route. However, at the T-junction mentioned above, cycle straight on and continue to a stop sign at the N4. Turn left onto the busy N4, signposted for Longford. Most of the road contains a hard shoulder that can be used to cycle on. Continue to a roundabout and take the first exit onto the R393 for Longford town centre. Near the town centre, follow the one-way system around to the left at St Mel's Cathedral. At the nearby T-junction, turn left to return to Longford train station nearby.

15. Longford-to-Cloondara Circuit

Longford – Killashee – Cloondara – Longford

Distance (km): 36	**Score:** ✳ ✳ ✳
Cycling Time (hours): 1¾–2¼	**Traffic:** 1
Grade: 1	**Train Station:** Longford
Gain: 59m	**Grid Reference:** N 134 749

This route meanders to Cloondara, close to where the Royal Canal ends its course from Dublin at the River Shannon. A mix of road and canal track makes this a pleasing and easy cycle with little traffic. There is also the chance of seeing some canal wildlife.

Cloondara, County Longford.

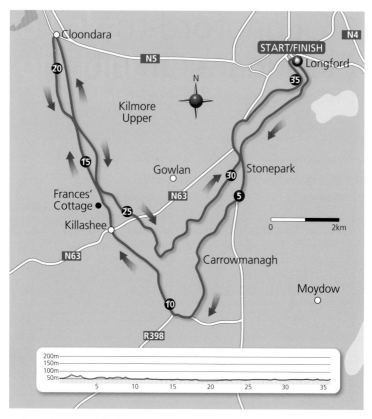

On exiting Longford train station car park, turn left over the railway track and follow the road as it veers to the right nearby. Cycle on to a cemetery near the junction with the R397 and turn left onto that road. Continue to a church about 5km from Longford. Turn right at the church onto the L5248. Continue to a Y-junction and keep left. The road eventually terminates at the R398. Turn right onto the R398 and cross over the canal on a new bridge (the old one is to the left). Take the nearby right-hand turn onto the L1148, signposted for Killashee.

At Ballynakill near Killashee was the site of an old monastery. Local folklore tells of an extraordinary bell that hung on an ash tree next to the monastery. It tolled beautifully when calling the monks to prayer as if a voice from heaven. During the reign of Henry VIII, the monastery was suppressed and the monks dispersed. The suppressors, having heard of the bell, took it to one of their own belfries. But when the rope was pulled, the bell was silent. Then one day, it broke from the belfry and soared through the air, tolling more beautifully than ever. Finally, it settled back on the tree next to the monastery where it continued to toll. When the monks failed to turn up for prayer, it broke from the tree and smashed to pieces on the ground.

Cycle on to a Y-junction in Killashee and bear left, following the signs for Cloondara and the L1162. Then turn right soon after onto the L1162, signposted for Cloondara. This is designated cycling route 1A. Cross over the canal at a lifting bridge and cycle through a boggy area. After cycling 19km from the train station, arrive at a junction in Cloondara (also called Clondra). There are information boards here on cycling, walking and canoeing. From here, the River Camlin and the Royal Canal later merge into the River Shannon.

Completed in 1817, the Royal Canal was a novel form of transport. Two classes of passenger boat were used, a fly boat and a night boat. Canal travel, though, did not appeal to Mr and Mrs Hall. They were travelling the country in 1843 and, on the way to Longford, described their canal experience:

Barges on the Royal Canal at Cloondara, County Longford.

Frances' Cottage by the Royal Canal, Killashee.

We entered the county by the Royal Canal, voyaging part of the way in one of the 'Fly-boats'. It is long and narrow; covered in as we see it; and there are two divisions for different classes of passengers. As a mode of travelling it is exceedingly inconvenient; there is scarcely space to turn in the confined cabin; and an outside 'berth' for more than one is impossible. The guide, or guard, takes his stand at the bow of the boat, and a helmsman controls its motions. It proceeds at a very rapid pace – about seven Irish miles an hour – drawn by two or three horses, who are made to gallop all the way. There is also a more cumbrous vessel, called a 'night boat', which travels at a much slower rate – about four miles an hour – and always at night. It is large, awkward, and lumbering, and is chiefly used by the peasantry on account of its cheapness.

At the junction in Cloondara, turn left over the canal. Take the canal-bank cycling track on this side, signposted Cycle 1A and Killashee. The track goes all the way to Longford. The quality varies but generally there is a good gritted surface. At Savage Bridge and Lock 44, stay on the canal bank and leave Cycle 1A as it takes the road. Pass Frances' Cottage adjacent to Lock 44. Built about 1840, the charming lock-keeper's cottage was refurbished in 1990 by American Frances K. Kelly.

Near Killashee, cross over the canal and continue on the left bank. Eventually, the track veers left away from the main canal onto the branch to Longford. This section is dry and the channel is filled with vegetation.

A lock on the Royal Canal.

At about 30km, cross the canal to the right bank. Continue to Longford, following the track's cycling/walking signs. On approaching Longford, the track narrows. Take extra care because the number of pedestrians increases. Eventually, arrive at a T-junction at a block of apartments and turn right. Continue to the next junction nearby and turn right again, following the sign to the train station located nearby.

There was a story told hereabouts of a farmer who was fed up with hard work and dreamt of easy money. After a night on the beer, he waddled home, thinking about how he would spend his easy money. As his mind was in the act of purchasing a new pony and trap, he heard singing from behind a lone bush. Sneaking up, he saw a leprechaun happily mending shoes. The farmer snatched the little man and demanded his crock of gold. The leprechaun tried all the tricks in his book to escape but the farmer was determined to get his easy fortune. Finally, the leprechaun pointed to a nearby rock and declared the gold was beneath it. Holding his prisoner in one hand, the farmer turned the rock with the other and there beneath it lay a fortune in gold sovereigns. In his effort to get it, he slipped and knocked his head. When he awoke his head was hazy from the bump and effects of the drink. The leprechaun had gone but the gold remained. Laughing out loud, he put his hands through the sovereigns, but there was no clinking, only the rustle of golden autumn leaves that had fallen from the lone bush.

16. Longford-to-Lake Gowna Figure of Eight

Longford – Aughnacliffe – Lough Gowna – Ballinalee – Longford

Distance (km): 69	**Score:** ✶ ✶ ✶
Cycling Time (hours): 3½–4	**Traffic:** 2
Grade: 4	**Train Station:** Longford
Gain: 639m	**Grid Reference:** N 134 749

Traversing counties Longford and Cavan, in Ulster, this route showcases the countryside of both counties. Lake and hill views are the reward, though the price is a couple of challenging climbs to work the lungs.

St Mel's Cathedral, Longford.

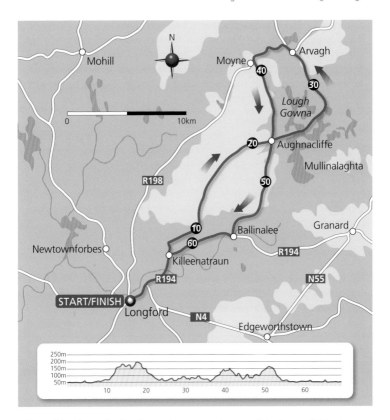

On exiting Longford train station car park, turn right towards the town centre. At the nearby traffic lights, turn right again and cycle to St Mel's Cathedral.

Construction started in 1840, but it was not until 1893 that St Mel's Cathedral was finally consecrated. The cathedral is called after St Mel, who accepted the Christian leadership role from St Patrick for this locality. A sculpture of the saint dominates above the cathedral portico. Disaster struck in 2009 when a fire devastated the building, to the dismay of the people of Longford. However, they rallied together and after a huge effort the cathedral was refurbished and reopened for worship in 2014.

At the cathedral, turn left, following the sign for the R194 and Ballinalee. Continue to a roundabout and take the second exit onto the R194. At the next roundabout take the first exit to stay on the R194. Cycle on to a crossroads at Killeenatruan and go straight onto the L1040 towards Aughnacliffe. On this road, the hills offer lovely views of the Longford countryside. Having cycled about 17km, you come to a junction with many signs. Follow the brown one towards Lough Gowna and go straight on to Aughnacliffe, about 22km from Longford. At the junction here, turn left, then right nearby, following the sign for Lough Gowna. At the crossroads with signage indicating Lough Gowna to the left, right and straight on, go straight on.

Local tales of the banshee of Lough Gowna have scared children for years. The mermaid-like creature would appear when a drowning was imminent. She has been described as having long, flowing hair and sits on the water, keening. Once she appears, a drowning can be expected. One such tragedy is the case of four men. After a day's shooting, they were partying on an iron yacht on Lough Gowna. In the early hours they decided to return to shore on a small punt. Three climbed safely from the yacht onto the punt but the fourth man fell from the ladder and overturned it. All four were thrown into the water and drowned. The banshee had been seen earlier near Inch Island where her eerie wail had predicted the tragedy.

At 28km from Longford, arrive at the village of Lough Gowna. The village was at one time called Scrabby but the villagers changed the name in the 1950s. At the crossroads in Lough Gowna, go straight on, following the sign for Arvagh. Soon after, take the left-hand turn signposted for Arvagh. Arriving at a junction on the outskirts of Arvagh, turn left towards the village centre. At the library turn left again, following the sign for Longford. At the nearby T-junction, turn right and follow the road as it veers left onto the R198 towards Moyne.

There was a story told hereabouts about a man who wasn't too fond of work. However, his well had collapsed and, having no water, he had to do something. So he took a pick and shovel and began to clear the blockage. He hadn't done much when the work got the better of him. So he sat down to rest and consider his position. Suddenly, he jumped up, stood the shovel in the ground and half buried the pick where he had started to dig. He proceeded to hang his coat and cap on the vertical shovel and then shuffled behind a ditch to wait. It wasn't long before a couple of men walked by and noticed the cap and coat and half-buried pick. On investigating, they reckoned that the well had collapsed on the man who owned the cap and coat. They began to dig furiously until the well was opened. The two were more than surprised when the owner of the cap and coat appeared to thank them for digging out the well. This local tale proves the old saying, 'Where there's a well there's a way'.

At the crossroads near Moyne, turn left onto the L1028, signposted for Aughnacliffe. Continue on this road to a T-junction at a shop and turn right towards Aughnacliffe, 2km away. While cycling through

The dolmen at Aughnacliffe, County Longford.

Aughnacliffe, keep an eye out for the Dolmen signpost on the left. This portal tomb dates to about 3,800 BC. The capstone appears to be balanced precariously and could have dire consequences for an itchy cow. Access to the monument is through a field. To continue, go straight on to Ballinalee.

Two soldiers-turned-politicians were associated with Ballinalee: the republican, General Seán Mac Eoin and the unionist, Field-Marshal Sir Henry Wilson. Mac Eoin's career began as a blacksmith and he inherited his father's blacksmith business. Wilson, on the other hand, was born into a wealthy Anglo-Irish family. As the second son, he was not entitled to inherit his father's estate and so gravitated towards an army career. Both were successful military men, Mac Eoin as an IRA commander

Statue of Seán McEoin, Ballinalee, County Longford.

View from the road to Ballinalee near Aughnacliffe

in the War of Independence and later head of the Irish army. Wilson rose through the ranks of the British army, with Lloyd George commenting that he 'was the greatest strategist we possess'. Wilson's career in British politics began promisingly but was cut short. The IRA assassinated him in 1922 outside his home in London. After Mac Eoin's army career, he too entered politics and served at ministerial level in the Irish government. Mac Eoin was more fortunate than Wilson: he just about escaped execution by the British during the War of Independence.

At the crossroads in Ballinalee, turn right onto the R194 signposted for Longford. Follow the R194 into Longford town. At St Mel's Cathedral, turn right at the stop sign and sign for the train station. Follow the one-way system to the T-junction and turn left to return to the train station nearby.

17. Lusk-to-Balrothery Loop

Lusk – Balrothery – Balbriggan – Skerries – Lusk

Distance (km): 29	**Score:** ✴ ✴ ✴ ✴
Cycling Time (hours): 1½–1¾	**Traffic:** 2
Grade: 1	**Train Station:** Rush/Lusk
Gain: 144m	**Grid Reference:** O 231 538

Follow part of the Dublin-to-Dunleer turnpike, an old toll road operating several centuries before the motorway version nearby, and that's only a fraction of this interesting and scenic route.

The Man of War pub, County Dublin.

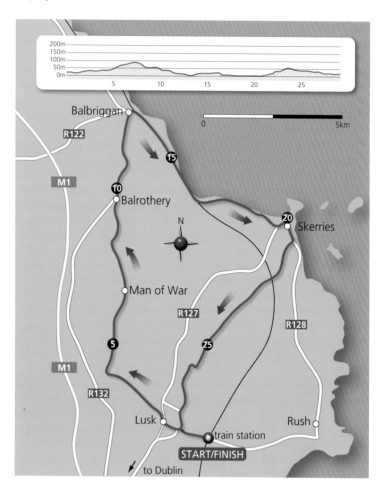

On exiting Rush/Lusk train station car park, turn left towards Lusk. At the nearby Remount roundabout, take the second exit towards the old church, which is merged with the round tower in the village.

Lusk is an ancient place where legends flourish. One relates to Cuchulainn, the Hound of Ulster. In search of a bride, he fell in love with Emer at Lusk. Emer's father, Fergal, had other plans. He wanted her to marry the King of Tara. So he tricked Cuchulainn's uncle into sending the young warrior away to hone his battle skills. However, Fergal was not as cunning as he thought. Cuchulainn and Emer had made a pact that they would only marry each other. Eventually, Cuchulainn returned and the two eloped to find happiness. Alas, not for long, for Cuchulainn was slain in battle, and Emer, devastated, died of a broken heart.

At the traffic lights in the centre of Lusk, turn right. Continue along Main Street and, after passing pedestrian lights, turn left onto Chapel Road. Cycle past the nearby church and then keep right, joining the road ahead. Continue on this road until you meet a junction at a grass triangle, about 4km from the railway station. Turn right onto this old turnpike road and stay on it until you reach the thatched Man of War pub, about 7km from the railway station.

Near the pub was the turnpike gate where you had to pay a toll to pass. The eighteenth-century toll system was complicated. There were twelve different toll rates, depending on the vehicle or animal passing through. A bicycle would have posed a problem for the attendant since it hadn't been invented then. It could not be classified as a coach, chaise, wagon or dray, and a horse, mare, gelding or donkey didn't pull it. You can imagine the head scratching! On the plus side, wearing Lycra pants wouldn't have been seen as strange since tight stockings were fashionable for both men and women at the time.

Flower display at Balrothery.

Railway viaduct at Balbriggan.

Pass the Man of War pub and continue straight on to Balrothery, 10km from the start.

In 1801, Lieutenant Joseph Archer described 'Balruddery' as a small fishing village, a rather strange observation since it is some distance from the sea. On a different tack, there is evidence of a Bronze Age settlement here, though Balrothery is better known as the 'Town of the Knights'. The village was an administration centre for Norman knights and there are the remains of an old castle here. Robert de Rosel was granted Balrothery in 1171. He built the town and castle.

On entering Balrothery, cycle through a mini-roundabout and pass the Balrothery Inn, another old pub established in 1656. Continue to a mini-roundabout and take the second exit. Soon after is a pedestrian/cycle track. Follow the cycle track to a roundabout and take the second exit into Balbriggan town centre, about 13km from the start. Cycle past the Bracken Court Hotel and, after passing the pedestrian lights at the hollow in the road, turn right onto Quay Street towards the harbour and the railway viaduct.

Balbriggan was world-famous for its textiles, introduced by the local landlord, Baron Hamilton. The textile firm Smith and Co., or Smyco, was in existence for 200 years from 1780. The firm supplied underclothing to the rich and famous. Queen Victoria loved her Balbriggan hose and wore it every day. One of the firm's employees, Thomas Mangan, made the queen's stockings for sixty years. They were of the finest silk or Sea Island cotton. Mangan's stockings were exhibited in Philadelphia in 1853 and regarded as the finest ever made. Victoria knew quality when she wore it. Smyco closed its doors in 1980, unable to compete with modern cheap imports.

Cycle under the rightmost arch of the viaduct and continue on this road all the way to Skerries; it becomes the R127. The coastal view towards Skerries is super. In Skerries you will come to a traffic-signalled T-junction. Turn left and follow the road to the obelisk known locally as the 'monument'. Take the second exit off the monument roundabout and cycle along Strand Street. Pass the church on the right. Take the first right-hand turn after a pub called the Malting House Inn. There is another church on the left and the entrance to Skerries Mills and café is on the right.

The three mills at Skerries consist of a five-sail windmill, a thatched four-sail windmill and a watermill. Recently restored, they are unique to this location where flour was milled from the twelfth century. The working mills are fine examples of seventeenth-, eighteenth- and nineteenth-century industrial engineering and demonstrate sustainability by the use of water and wind power. There is also a pond at the mills' entrance that abounds with wildlife. In early summer, a pair of swans and their cygnets may be seen. The young cygnets are sometimes carried on a parent's back. Ducks and moorhen also have their home here, while its common for a variety of gulls to swoop over the pond in search of titbits.

Continue straight on, passing through a crossroads to leave Skerries behind. After covering about 24km, arrive at a staggered crossroads by a farm. Turn right and then immediately left. Continue to a junction about 26km from the start and turn left onto Commons Lane. Follow this twisting road to a T-junction. Turn left onto Raheny Lane and cycle to a T-junction at the Lusk ring road. Turn left onto the ring road in the direction of Rush. At the nearby Raheny roundabout, take the second exit. The next roundabout is called Remount, which was met at the start. Take the first exit towards Rush. Continue until you come to Rush/ Lusk railway station on the right.

18. Lusk-to-Garristown Loop

Lusk – Ballyboughal – Oldtown – Garristown – Lusk

Distance (km): 42	**Score:** ✳ ✳ ✳
Cycling Time (hours): 2–2½	**Traffic:** 2
Grade: 2	**Train Station:** Rush/Lusk
Gain: 220m	**Grid Reference:** O 231 538

Though close to the busy capital, the sleepy villages of Garristown and Oldtown have managed to escape the city's encroachment, making them a retreat for cyclists. In comparison, the population of Lusk has exploded in recent years, yet it still manages to retain its village aspect.

Church and tower, Lusk, County Dublin.

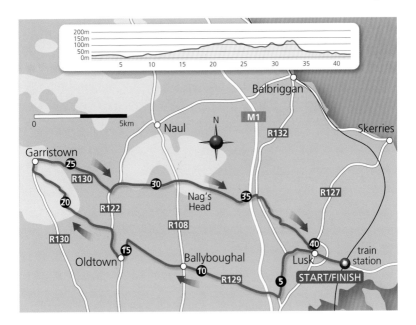

On exiting the railway station, turn left towards Lusk. At the nearby Remount roundabout, take the second exit and cycle towards the old church and round tower in the centre of Lusk. At the traffic lights in the centre, cross to the opposite side and turn left onto Church Road (which is more of a lane). Cycle the short distance to a stop sign and swing right, which will take you towards the unusual complex of the nineteenth-century church merged with a fifteenth-century fortification and a ninth-century round tower.

Believe it or not, Lusk was said to be a port, which is odd, because the village is some distance from the sea. However, the origin of this goes back to Viking times when longboats sailed into nearby Rogerstown Estuary. When the black raven sails were spotted, the alarm was raised. Panic ensued and the Lusk monks hitched up their habits and scampered to the safety of the round tower, now attached to a nineteenth-century church and a fifteenth-century fortification. They'd secure the tower and pray till the Viking horde got bored and went off to pillage somewhere else. The round tower has outlasted the monks, the Vikings and much more since and will probably dominate Lusk for another thousand years.

Pass the old church and tower and continue to a T-junction at the R132, 3.5km from the train station. Turn left onto the R132 towards Swords. Continue on this road until you come to a junction signposted

103

Taking a break at Ballyboughal.

for Ballyboughal. Turn right onto the R129 towards the village. At Ballyboughal, turn left over the bridge, then immediately right, to stay on the R129, signposted for Oldtown and Garristown. Continue towards Oldtown, passing a 1798 memorial on the right. About 14km from the start, turn left at a T-junction into Oldtown. At the next T-junction in the village, turn right onto the R122 towards Naul.

On 15 January 1947, on a cold winter's evening, the little community hall in Oldtown was packed. On stage sat the leading citizens, the parish priest and senior ESB people. The event was the switching-on of electricity to the village, the first in Ireland to be connected to the Rural Electrification Scheme, now known as the Quiet Revolution. But things were not going well. Storms had caused a last-minute glitch and there was a fault in the supply line. An ESB man was giving a speech to the eager crowd. He glanced frequently at a dormant gramophone. Its operation would signal the supply was back. He was running out of things to say when the turntable began to rotate and the strains of 'Cockles and Mussels' filled the hall. The supply was back. Wiping sweat from his brow, the ESB man watched a big switch being thrown. The hall and village were immersed in a blaze of light and the oil lamp was consigned to a page in history.

Continue towards Naul. At about 17km from the railway station, there is a sign at a crossroads indicating Ballyboughal to the right. Turn left instead and continue to a nearby crossroads, where you go straight across. At the next junction, turn right, following the sign for Garristown,

A ruined church, near Oldtown, County Dublin.

5km away. Continue to a T-junction and turn right, followed by the next left, signposted for Garristown. Arrive on the outskirts of the village at a junction with the R130. Swing right into the village. Garristown is about 23km from Rush/Lusk station.

In 1745, Garristown was a remote part of Fingal, not unlike today. Back then, illegal distilling was so prevalent that the authorities appointed a local excise man or 'gauger' to seize stills and illegal liquor. However, the job wasn't easy. In 1757, a gauger named Burleigh found concealed pot ale and other liquors in the house of Brian Crosbie. Under Crosbie's direction, a mob assembled and attacked Burleigh with staves and stones. He suffered serious cuts, bruises and a broken leg. Another gauger, Henry Daniel, was so frightened he couldn't do his job. He said the place was completely lawless and a guard of soldiers was needed to accompany him. Soldiers were often called to support the excise men over the twenty years or so that the gaugers were employed here. During this time, the residents continued to thwart the efforts of the authorities. The locals were certainly a robust bunch, except, perhaps in respect of their livers.

In the centre of Garristown turn right onto the R130 in the direction of Naul. At about 28km from the start, turn left at a junction onto the R122 and continue towards Naul. Soon after, swing right onto the L1070, signposted for Lusk. Cycle uphill to a crossroads at the R108 and go across onto the L1080 towards Lusk, 10km away. A short climb takes you to the hilltop and crossroads at the Nag's Head.

Hollywood graveyard is close by on the right, just before a left-hand turn to a quarry. The entrance gate is easily missed. There are ruins of a medieval church and Hollywood may have been a site of ancient royals. The place is very peaceful and a chorus of birdsong enhances the experience of the fine views. From the Nag's Head, there are views of the coast, Lambay Island, Howth Head and the Dublin and Wicklow mountains. The mountains seem to emerge from the sea to creep westwards like a serpent. On a clear day, you can see the red-and-white smokestacks of the old Poolbeg power station near the mouth of the River Liffey.

Continue on to enjoy the steep run downhill. Near the bottom, cross over the M1 to a nearby roundabout. Take the third exit to cross over the R132 and then the second exit off the second roundabout to a stop sign. Turn right in the direction of the Man of War pub. Eventually you arrive at a T-junction. Turn right. Soon after, take the left-hand turn onto Quickpenny Road at the junction with a grass triangle. Quickpenny Road leads to Lusk. At the church in Lusk (not the one with the round tower), keep right on the triangle and then veer left onto Post Office Road. Arrive at a T-junction opposite a supermarket and turn right. At the nearby traffic lights, veer left, following the sign for the railway station. At the Remount roundabout, take the second exit towards Rush and continue to the railway station situated on the right.

Looking south towards the Dublin and Wicklow mountains from the medieval church at Hollywood, Nag's Head, County Dublin.

19. Maynooth-to-Athboy Loop

Maynooth – Summerhill – Athboy – Ballivor – Maynooth

Distance (km): 110	**Score:** ✳ ✳
Cycling Time (hours): 5–6	**Traffic:** 2
Grade: 3	**Train Station:** Maynooth
Gain: 233m	**Grid Reference:** N 938 373

Though long, this route is quite easy and there are few hills to contend with. Panoramic views are somewhat limited, but the local roads are quiet and offer a relaxing cycle. Donadea Forest Park is worth a visit if time allows.

The eighteenth-century church of St Michael's and All Angels, Rathmolyon, County Meath.

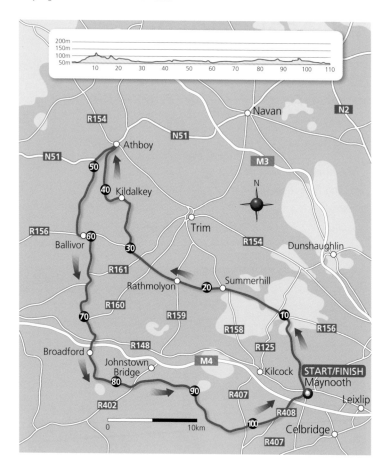

Exit Maynooth train station car park and turn left to Maynooth town centre. At the signalled T-junction, turn left and then right towards Kilcock on the R148. Rather than following the R148 around to the left by the nearby church, go straight onto a local road away from the traffic. At the junction about 7km from the station, keep to the main road, signposted for Dunboyne. At the following T-junction, turn left onto the R156, signposted for Summerhill. Continue to the roundabout near Summerhill and take the second exit into the town centre.

Elisabeth, Empress of Austria, visited Summerhill in 1879 on a hunting trip. If you are looking for a few beauty tips, she is your woman. Obsessed with beauty, Empress Elisabeth lived on a diet of meat juice, fresh milk from cows that accompanied her on her travels and egg whites mixed with salt.

She slept with hot towels around her waist and had her riding costumes sewn on to emphasis its tiny size. Treatment for her complexion consisted of purified honey and an ointment of strawberries crushed in Vaseline. As for her hair, she had it washed in a concoction of cognac, onions and Peruvian balsam. The newspapers of the time loved her and filled pages on her eccentricities.

Follow the road through the centre of Summerhill, passing the shady village green. At nearby pedestrian lights, turn left onto the R156 for Rathmolyon. Stay on the R156 through Rathmolyon towards Ballivor. Cross the R160, followed by the R161, to stay on the R156. After crossing the slow-moving River Boyne, arrive at a nearby T-junction and turn right onto the L4021 signposted for Trim. Soon after, turn left onto the L4015 following the sign for Kildalkey. This road terminates at a T-junction and turning left will take you into Kildalkey. Follow the road through and beyond Kildalkey. Having cycled 38km, take the right-hand turn signposted for Delvin. At the following crossroads, there are no signposts. However, turn right, which is in the direction of Athboy. Continue on this rough bog road to where it terminates at a junction with the N51. Turn right into Athboy which is about 45km from the start.

Athboy's origins extend back to the sixth century AD. It began as a settlement at the river crossing known as the Yellow Ford. The earliest inhabitants were druids who settled at the nearby Hill of Ward. During the

Near Athboy, County Meath.

late twelfth century, the Anglo-Normans occupied Athboy and by 1497 the town was granted a charter by the English King Henry VII. After the Irish defeat by Cromwell in the mid-seventeeth century, much of the land in the Athboy area passed to his supporters. One John Bligh acquired large estates and the family was later given the title Earl of Darnley. Over the years, the Darnleys developed the town and were responsible for its much of its layout today.

From Athboy, take the N51 towards Devlin. At a pitch-and-putt course, turn left onto the L8006, signposted for Higginstown. Continue to a crossroads and go straight across, following the sign for Ballivor. Eventually, arrive at a T-junction with the R156. Turn left onto the R156 into Ballivor.

Clonycavan Man was discovered at a bog near Ballivor in 2003. He was a healthy young man who lived during the Iron Age. Unfortunately, when his remains were found, the lower part of his body was missing. It was probably dismembered in a peat-cutting machine and this was on top of his own violent death all those years ago. His skull had been split open by what was probably a stone axe and his nose shattered by the same instrument. To make matters worse, the unfortunate young man had had his nipples sliced off, an indication perhaps of a royal background. One theory is that in ancient Ireland sucking a king's nipples was a gesture of submission and so slicing them off would have removed that symbolic power. His killing was sacrificial and he was probably kneeling while facing his executioner. He now rests in the National Museum along with his fellow 'bog men', Oldcroghan, Gallagh and Baronstown West.

On entering Ballivor, turn right onto the L4016 signposted for Kinnegad. The L4016 terminates at the R161. Cycle straight onto it towards Kinnegad. At about 65km, take the left-hand turn onto the L80301, signposted for Longwood. Arrive at a T-junction and turn right for Clonard. Cross the Royal Canal and railway side by side and take the left turn immediately after. Continue to a T-junction, keeping left towards Longwood. At a nearby crossroads, go straight onto the R160, signposted for Edenderry. The R160 soon terminates at the R148. Turn right onto the R148 and take the immediate left off it. Follow the road over the M4 motorway into the neat village of Broadford.

Cycle through Broadford and continue through a set of crossroads in the direction of Edenderry. After the crossroads, take the left-hand turn about 78km from the start. It is not signposted. Follow this road to a T-junction with the R402. Turn left and then right, following the sign for Donadea. Continue to a stop sign at a T-junction and turn right. There are no signposts. At the next T-junction, by the entrance to Knockvalley Golf club, turn right. Follow the signs for Donadea to a

Maynooth Castle, a fifteenth-century stronghold of the FitzGeralds, the Earls of Kildare.

crossroads at a pub decorated with flowers. Turn left and pass Donadea Forest Park.

Donadea Forest Park covers 240 hectares of mixed broadleaf and conifer woodland. Remains of its past social history still exist. Donadea Castle was the home of the Aylmer family. The park also boasts walled gardens, a church, icehouse, boathouse and a lime-tree avenue. There is a lake filled with waterfowl and flora, and a bite can be enjoyed in the café.

Continue to a junction where the main road veers to the right. Cycle onto the minor road ahead, signposted for the North Kildare Tourist Route. Cross the R407 onto the L1010 towards Maynooth. At the next crossroads by a church, turn left onto the R408 for Maynooth. Continue to a stop sign in the town and turn left. Follow the road, passing the entrance to the university and the Geraldine castle, to traffic lights. Cross the junction and turn right at the next signalled junction, following the sign for Celbridge. Continue to the entrance of the railway station on the right at the pedestrian lights.

20. Maynooth-to-Edenderry Figure of Eight

Maynooth – Carbury – Edenderry – Clane – Maynooth

Distance (km): 96	**Score:** ✷ ✷ ✷
Cycling Time (hours): 4½–5	**Traffic:** 2
Grade: 3	**Train Station:** Maynooth
Gain: 187m	**Grid Reference:** N 938 373

Though quite long, this is an easy cycle through flat peatland in counties Kildare and Offaly. The Bog of Allen offers a diverse Irish landscape where bogs, once exploited for turf, are now providing ecotourism opportunities.

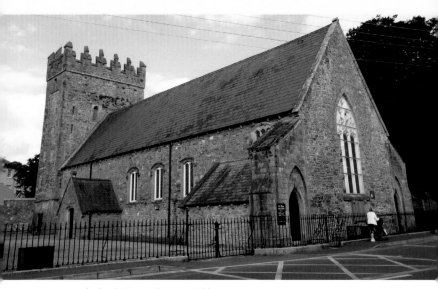

St Mary's Church, Maynooth, County Kildare.

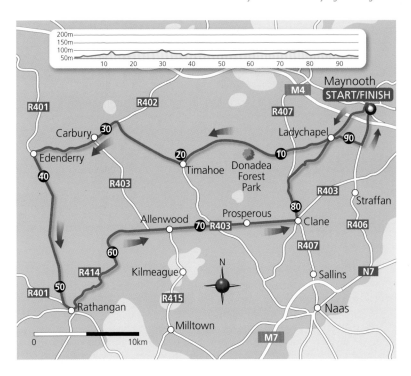

On exiting Maynooth train station car park, turn left to the town centre. Arrive at a signalled T-junction and turn left again. At the next signalled junction, cycle across towards the castle and veer left, passing the university entrance. Continue on and, after crossing the Royal Canal, turn right on the R408, signposted for Rathcoffey. After 5km, arrive at Ladychapel crossroads by a large church. Turn right at the church onto the L1010 towards Donadea Forest Park. Cycle to the crossroads with the R407 and cross it, following the sign for Donadea. Continue to a stop sign at a junction and go straight on. After 12km, pass the wooded entrance to Donadea Forest Park, followed by the old castellated entrance.

Now owned by the state, Donadea was originally in the hands of the Aylmer family for about 400 years. The family was involved with the various conflicts of the turbulent seventeenth century and the Aylmer women didn't shy away from doing their bit. During the Rebellion of 1641, the rebel Andrew Aylmer, 2nd Baronet of Donadea, was imprisoned. An army was dispatched to take Donadea Castle. Ellen Aylmer, Andrew's sister, was no pushover. However, despite her best efforts, the castle was taken and burned. She subsequently rebuilt it. During the Jacobite–Williamite War

Carbury Castle, Carbury, County Kildare.

of the late seventeenth century, Lady Ellen Aylmer was in charge. She was the widow of the 3rd Baronet and found herself outlawed because of her support for King James II. However, the wily woman managed to hold on to the estate under the terms of the Treaty of Limerick.

Cycle on from Donadea to Gilltown Bog and then enter the village of Timahoe. At an old hand pump by a seat, turn right, following the sign for Carbury. Eventually arrive at a junction with the R402 by a thatched cottage looking like it is half buried. Turn left to Carbury by following the sign for Edenderry. Near Carbury is a view of Carbury Castle, a ruined Tudor mansion on the Hill of Carbury. The R402 arrives at a roundabout bypassing the well-kept village itself. Take the second exit onto the R402 and continue to Edenderry, 6km away.

Shortly after D-Day (6 June 1944), an American Air Force pilot found himself upside down in a bog near Edenderry. A group of turf workers were beavering away at Clonsast Bog when a large plane thundered overhead as it prepared for a forced landing. The pilot thought he was landing on a smooth surface but the wheels dug into the bog and his plane flipped over. The turf workers helped free the pilot and he was taken to the Curragh Camp. However, unlike lost German and British pilots who were detained, the American was brought to the border and handed over. The pilot, called Iris Dillon, returned to the United States and enjoyed a successful career in the Air Force. It was a happy ending to a near-fatal tragedy.

In the centre of Edenderry, turn left onto the L1001 towards Rathangan. Pass under the Blundell Aqueduct, carrying the Grand Canal, and follow the straight, level bog road where cut turf is laid out to dry in

Railway line through bog near Edenderry, County Offaly.

summer. At the outskirts of Rathangan, arrive at a roundabout. Take the first exit into the town centre and when there, turn left onto the R414, following the sign for Lullymore. Continue on the R414, passing Lullymore Heritage and Discovery Park and the Bog of Allen Nature Centre. These centres provide information about biodiversity and the use of peatlands. Cycle on to the Shee humpback bridge over the Grand Canal and turn right onto the R403, signposted for Allenwood.

There was a story told hereabouts of an old farmer who made a will influenced by his scheming cousins. He didn't own much but he had a good plough horse and a mangy dog. His long-suffering wife hoped to be looked after in the will. When the man died and his will was read, the poor woman got the shock of her life. His will stated the plough horse and the dog should be sold. The money made from the horse would go to the scheming cousins and the money from the dog would go to her. Thinking on her feet, she rushed to the market and called out. 'Who will buy a dog for twenty pounds and a horse for a shilling? The only stipulation,' she continued, 'is that they must be bought together.' As the horse was worth more than the two combined, she soon got a sale and a receipt showing the sale price of each. The £20 went into her own pocket and, with a generous smile, she gave the cousins the shilling.

Pass through Allenwood staying on the R403 to arrive at Prosperous, about 76km from the start.

The 1798 Rebellion was a nasty affair, as both sides could be merciless. The first military action of the rebellion began at Prosperous in May 1798 when the United Irishmen attacked the British garrison there. The

Royal Canal at Shee Bridge near Allenwood, County Offaly.

garrison consisted of about sixty soldiers and militia. Captain Swayne, the commander, had made himself unpopular by terrorising the locals. Dr John Esmond and Andrew Farrell led about 500 United Irishmen into the town at night. After the sentries were dispensed with and the gates of the barracks opened, they forced their way into Swayne's quarters and he was piked and shot. The barracks was set on fire and many who tried to escape were piked in the streets. Nearly forty soldiers and militia were killed and Swayne's body was burnt in a tar barrel. However, over thirty Irish prisoners at Dunlavin in County Wicklow were massacred in an act of revenge. A Colonel Stewart and his military retook Prosperous about a month later and also showed little mercy.

Pass through Prosperous and continue to Clane. Near the centre of town, turn left at the traffic lights. The old church tower is opposite. Continue straight through town and onto a cycle lane towards Maynooth. Pass the castellated entrance to Clongowes Wood College and arrive at a junction with the R408. Turn right towards Maynooth. Cycle through the village of Rathcoffey and stay on the R408 towards Maynooth. At Ladychapel crossroads by the large church, turn right onto the L5037 towards Maynooth. Pass the ancient monastic site of Taghadoe to reach a junction with the R406 and turn left onto it. Continue towards Maynooth and at a roundabout take the second exit. Cycle on to the railway station on the left.

21. Maynooth-to-Tara Loop

Maynooth – Kilcock – Summerhill – Tara – Dunsany – Maynooth

Distance (km): 75	**Score:** ★ ★ ★
Cycling Time (hours): 3½–4	**Traffic:** 2
Grade: 2	**Train Station:** Maynooth
Gain: 342m	**Grid Reference:** N 938 373

This pleasant route into legendary Meath will require some hill work. However, it's worth it. The Hill of Tara includes a number of ancient monuments and is said to be the seat of the High King of Ireland. It was also a sacred and mythical Celtic place.

Royal Canal, Kilcock, County Kildare.

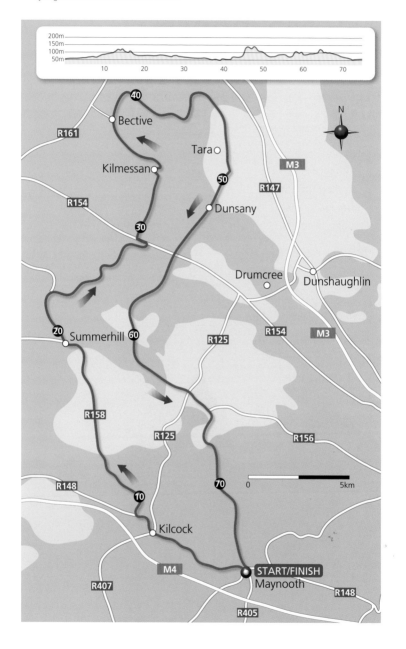

Exit Maynooth train station car park and turn left to Maynooth town centre. Continue to the signalled T-junction and turn left followed by a right at the next signalled junction towards Kilcock on the R148. Veer left at the church, following the sign for Kilcock. Cycle to a roundabout and take the second exit to continue to Kilcock. As you enter the town, the Royal Canal leads the way. At the T-junction by a canal bridge, turn right through the town. Follow the road around to the left and continue to the junction for Summerhill. Turn right here onto the R158 and at the nearby roundabout, take the first exit to continue to Summerhill.

On a tour of Ireland in the 1770s, the agricultural writer Arthur Young took the road to Summerhill from Maynooth. He described it as follows: 'The country is cheerful and rich; and if the Irish cabins continue like what I have hereto seen, I shall not hesitate to pronounce their inhabitants as well off as most English cottagers. They are built of mud wall 18 inches or 2 feet thick and well thatched, which are far warmer than the clay walls in England. Here, are few cottars without a cow and sometimes two, a belly full invariably of potatoes and generally turf for fuel from a bog. It is true they have not always chimneys to their cabins, the door serving for that and window too. Every cottage swarms with poultry and most of them have pigs.' How times have changed!

Arrive at a roundabout on the outskirts of Summerhill and take the first exit into this heritage town, about 18km from the start. In the centre, follow the road to the right on the R158, signposted for Trim. Continue out of the town on the R158 and after cycling about 21km, turn right at the sign for Kilmessan. Continue to a Y-junction and keep right, signposted for Kiltale. Cycle into Kiltale and to a T-junction with the R154.

Summerhill, County Meath.

There was a story told hereabouts of a young hunchback who was content with his lot. One day he was asked by his mother to collect kindling for the fire. As he collected the sticks, he sang like a thrush, as he often did. So sweet was his song that the fairies in a fort nearby came out, dancing and clapping. In appreciation of his singing, they took the hump from his back. Delighted with his straightness, he ran home and word soon spread. A humpy grumpy old crone heard of the boy's good fortune and slunk off to the fairy fort herself. As she picked up sticks, she sang like an old crow with a bad head cold. Soon the fairies came out of the fort covering their ears and then quickly ran back in. After the crone had finished, she took out a mirror to look at her back. To her consternation, she had two humps. The fairies had added the boy's.

Cycling into Kilmessan, County Meath.

Turn left onto the R154 and soon after turn right at a crossroads onto the L62034 towards Kilmessan. As you enter this pretty village, turn right at the T-junction after passing over an old railway bridge. Continue on, passing the entrance to the Station House Hotel. Cycle on to Bective crossroads and turn right at the pub here, following the sign for Duleek. Take the first turn to the right, about 38km from the start. Then turn left at a T-junction, following a sign indicating that Tara is 3km. Cycle to the next junction and turn right at another sign indicating Tara is 4km. Worry not: the route is not going backwards. At the next junction, turn right, following the sign for Tara, indicating 1km. Cycle up the Hill of Tara to the visitor centre, about 45km from the start. There is also a popular coffee shop here if sustenance is required.

Between 1899 and 1902, members of the influential British-Israel Association attempted to excavate the Hill of Tara. These eccentrics believed they'd find the Ark of the Covenant, the chest containing the stone tablets on which the finger of God had inscribed the Ten Commandments. Their work provoked a protest from people such as William Butler Yeats, Douglas Hyde and Maud Gonne. The press supported the protests, making it one of the earliest media campaigns to save a national monument. Eventually, the protesters succeeded. However, protests in recent times were not as successful when advocates of the M3 motorway succeeded in ploughing a route through the area.

Pass the visitor centre and continue downhill to the crossroads. Turn right following the sign for Dunsany.

Edward Plunkett, 18th Baron of Dunsany, was never short of a word. He was a prolific writer and dramatist, notable for his work in fantasy. He published under the name Lord Dunsany and his work consisted of around eighty books, hundreds of short stories, successful plays and essays. His ink bill must have been huge.

Continue through the crossroads at Dunsany to another set at the R154 and go straight across, following the sign for Summerhill. Cycle to yet another crossroads and turn left, following the sign for Kilcock. Continue to a T-junction and turn left onto the R156, signposted for Dunboyne. After climbing a hill, cycle through a crossroads and at the next junction turn right, following the sign for Maynooth, 8km away. At the nearby T-junction, keep left for Maynooth. Follow the signs to Maynooth and eventually, after passing a big church near the town centre, arrive at the signalled T-junction in the centre. Turn left here, followed by the next right, signposted for Celbridge. Continue to the train station entrance on the right.

Looking east from the Hill of Tara.

121

22. Mullingar-to-Abbeyshrule (Royal Canal West) Figure of Eight

Mullingar – Milltown – Abbeyshrule – Ballynacarrigy – Mullingar

Distance (km): 55	**Score:** ✳ ✳ ✳
Cycling Time (hours): 2¾–3¼	**Traffic:** 2
Grade: 2	**Train Station:** Mullingar
Gain: 118m	**Grid Reference:** N 433 527

Cycle to Abbeyshrule by road, returning by canal track and enjoy what the Royal Canal has to offer on this easy route through counties Westmeath and Longford. For those interested in wildlife there are opportunities to observe canal flora and fauna.

The mid-nineteenth-century belfry at St Mary's Church, Milltown, County Westmeath.

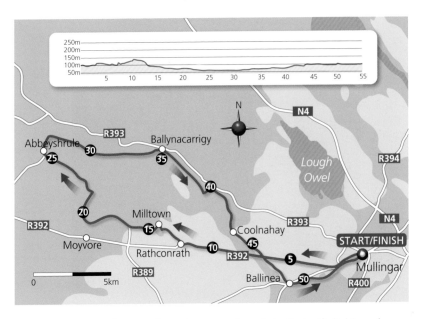

On exiting Mullingar train station car park, cycle to the traffic lights and turn left. Continue straight through the next set of lights on the R390, signposted for Athlone. After 2km, arrive at a roundabout and take the second exit onto the R392, signposted for Ballymahon. Continue on the R392 to Rathconrath, 12km from Mullingar, and then turn right onto the L5904 signposted for Milltown. Stay on this road, following the signs for Moyvore. Pass through Milltown and continue to a staggered crossroads. Cycle straight through, following the signpost for Moyvore. After the crossroads, take the second right leaving the Moyvore road. There is no signposting here but it is about 19km from the start.

Moyvore became a target for the infamous Lieutenant Edward Hepenstall, also known as 'the Walking Gallows'. It was about 1797 when the United Irishmen were preparing for rebellion that Hepenstall and his militia applied their methods to flush them out. Hepenstall's personal choice was to knock his victim half conscious with his considerable fist, tie a noose around the neck of the victim and, throwing the other end of the rope over his shoulder, drag the unfortunate until he was half hanged. If a confession was not forthcoming, he would finish the job. Judge, jury and executioner in Moyvore, he had an elderly blacksmith and his three sons killed for allegedly making pikes and then had the bodies dragged behind a cart. Some time later, he set fire to the village. The houses being thatched and the weather dry, the village was soon in ashes.

On the road towards Moyvore.

Continue on this road passing through the wooded areas of mainly evergreen trees. Eventually, arrive at a stop sign at a Y-junction and turn left. The road has grass in the centre until a crossroads. Cycle straight through the crossroads, following a small brown sign for Abbeyshrule. Continue to a Y-junction at a cemetery and turn right into Abbeyshrule, a Tidy Towns winner. The village is 26km from Mullingar train station.

The paradox that was Oliver Goldsmith was born in Pallas near Abbeyshrule about 1728. It was said that he was a genius with the pen and foolish without it. His academic and occupational careers were far from outstanding. He studied theology, law and medicine with some success and worked at various jobs, including education and busking (he played the flute). Goldsmith's personality was a contradiction and he seemed perpetually disorganised. He once planned to emigrate to America but

The bridge at Abbeyshrule, County Longford.

missed the boat. On another occasion after arriving in Edinburgh, he went off to check out the city without noting the name of his lodgings or the street it was on. Financially, he was in dire straits until his novel *The Vicar of Wakefield* was published and even with success his finances remained somewhat in disarray. He died prematurely in 1774 of a kidney complication that, apparently, he himself misdiagnosed.

Cross over the River Inny and continue through Abbeyshrule to the canal bridge. Cross the bridge and keep right onto the cycle track. Nearby is Whitworth Aqueduct.

About 55 metres long, Whitworth Aqueduct carries the Royal Canal over the River Inny. John Killaly, the engineer responsible for the Royal Canal between Coolnahay and Cloondara, designed this fine structure. The contractors were Henry, Mullins and McMahon. It took three years to build and cost £5,000. It is named after Lord Charles Whitworth, Lord Lieutenant of Ireland at the time. The aqueduct is in excellent condition, a testament to the quality and skill of the stonemasons and engineers involved. The limestone used may have come from a quarry at Castlewilder, located nearby.

Cross the aqueduct and follow the track through open bog, passing a number of canal bridges that lead nowhere. Later, Kelly's Bridge

125

The start of the Royal Canal cycling track at Abbeyshrule.

must be crossed to take up the track on the opposite side to get to Ballynacarrigy.

There was a story told hereabouts of man who went to sea to see the world. His travelling led to a life of debauchery and sin. Eventually his decadent life caught up with him and he died on board a ship that was carrying coal. As he was to be buried at sea, the captain ordered that his shroud be filled with coal so his body would sink to the bottom. As the sailors gathered to say their final farewell before tipping him overboard, one remarked, 'Things must be bad in Hell when Pat has to bring his own fuel.'

Leave Ballynacarrigy and cycle to Lock 32 at Kill Bridge. This is the halfway point on the canal track. From here, Abbeyshrule and Mullingar are equidistant at 12.5km. As I continued, I came across a heron and, unusually, a red squirrel on the track. The native red squirrel is much smaller than its foreign cousin, the grey squirrel, resulting in the smaller rodent losing out. Continue following the cycle signs to Mullingar, crossing the canal where indicated. As you approach the town, the railway station comes into view. There is an exit from the cycle track near the station.

23. Mullingar-to-Athlone (Old Rail Trail) Figure of Eight

Mullingar – Moyvoughly – Mount Temple – Athlone – Moate – Mullingar

Distance (km): 95	**Score:** ✶ ✶ ✶
Cycling Time (hours): 4½–5	**Traffic:** 1
Grade: 3	**Train Station:** Mullingar
Gain: 428m	**Grid Reference:** N 433 527

About half of this route is on the Old Rail Trail from Mullingar to Athlone and is an ideal track for novices and families. The surface is excellent and there is no great hardship involved. However, the road section will require some hill work.

Sign for the annual Bealtaine fire festival held at the Hill of Uisneach near Ballinea, County Westmeath.

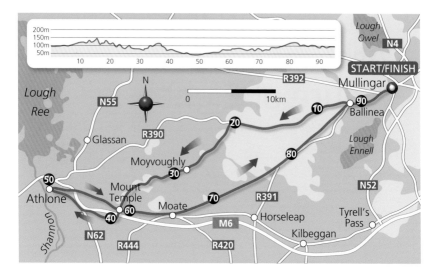

The entrance to the Royal Canal cycling and pedestrian track is opposite the train station car park exit. Once on the track, follow the sign towards Ballinea. Exit the track at Old Ballinea Bridge and veer right onto the R390. Cycle through Ballinea and continue on the R390, signposted for Athlone. Pass the Hill of Uisneach on the right, an ancient sacred site. After cycling 20km, turn left at a crossroads onto the L5338. Cycle straight on, following signs for Moate. Continue to the small community of Moyvoughly, about 28km from Mullingar.

Start of Old Rail Trail at Athlone.

It was around Moyvoughly that persons unknown murdered a member of a Westmeath bardic family and his wife. Owny O'Coffey was regarded as the most learned poet in Ireland when he was murdered in 1556. His surviving works include a long poem in praise of James Butler, ninth Earl of Ormond, and a theological piece that is 160 verses long. The celebrity bards of the time held positions of importance in the social order. Most influential Gaelic families sponsored a bard. His job was to compose verse in praise of his patron and embellish his patrons' best qualities, even if he was short of them.

On the far side of Moyvoughly is a Y-junction. Keep right here onto the minor road, signposted for Mount Temple. There are two more Y-junctions after, veer left at the first and right at the second, following the sign for Mount Temple. At the T-junction in the village turn right. After passing the church and golf club, take the next left and enjoy the views from this elevated road. Eventually arrive at a crossroads with the R446. Turn right onto the R446 towards Athlone. Follow the road into the busy town centre for a break and to view the mighty River Shannon.

Former railway station at Moate, County Westmeath.

In the depths of the National Museum rests a curious stone image of Peter Lewys, a bridge builder. What makes it curious is a rat creeping along the barrel of Lewys's drawn pistol. The current bridge in Athlone spanning the Shannon was built in 1844, replacing a former structure on which the stone image was mounted. Finished in 1567, the former bridge was commissioned by Sir Henry Sidney who appointed Peter Lewys as supervisor. Lewys was a clergyman as well as a bridge builder. It was said that he had changed religion, from Catholic to Protestant, and had been followed by a righteous rat ever since. When Lewys preached, the rat glared at him with piercing red eyes. One day, after delivering one of his more spirited sermons, the rat's glaring got to him. Drawing his pistol, he aimed at the creature. But the wily rat leapt onto the weapon and bit Lewys's trigger finger. The bite gave Lewys lockjaw, thus ending his preaching and, indeed, his life, for he died soon after.

Cycle back out of Athlone on the same road (R446) to a mini-roundabout and exit left, following the brown sign for the Old Rail Trail. Cross over a railway track and, at a mini-roundabout, take the second exit, signposted for the Old Rail Trail. Arrive at another railway bridge and turn left over it into a cul-de-sac. The Old Rail Trail starts here and the distance to Mullingar is 40km. The trail surface is excellent and if you fancy a break along the way, the old station at Moate has a coffee shop.

The completion of the Dublin-to-Galway line in 1851 saw the first passengers at Moate Station. The station served until 1973 when many of the Galway services were transferred through Portarlington. However, the station got a reprieve in the late 1970s. It became a film set for *The First Great Train Robbery* starring Sean Connery, Lesley-Anne Down and Donald Sutherland. Loosely based on an actual train robbery in Victorian England, it was written and directed by Michael Crichton (who also wrote *Jurassic Park*). The film won an Edgar Award for Best Motion Picture Screenplay. It is unlikely that this accolade had anything to do with Moate Station remaining open to some services until the 1980s and now it may come out of retirement to service the cycling route.

The next station after Moate is Castletown. It closed in 1963 after more than a hundred years' service. After cycling 92km, arrive at a modern overhead bridge. Keep left here onto the canal track, following the sign for cycle routes 1, 2 and 3. Follow the canal track to Mullingar railway station.

The nineteenth century brought big changes to the community and economy in Mullingar. The town was already a road hub from east to west and an important staging post for horse-drawn vehicles. Then came the opening of the Royal Canal in the early 1800s. The large barges could carry more people and goods than a coach or cart. The railway followed in 1848, causing a revolution in the speed of transporting people and goods. Gas lighting and a telegraph office introduced in the 1850s further enhanced commercial activity. The military also added to economic growth. Many British army regiments were stationed in the town and soldiers married local women and settled down. The army also provided employment, giving locals the opportunity to serve all over the British Empire. Mullingar continues to prosper and today is a thriving business, administrative and industrial centre.

River Shannon at Athlone, County Westmeath, with the Church of Ss Peter and Paul on the right.

24. Mullingar-to-Lilliput Loop

Mullingar – Multyfarnham – Lilliput – Ballinea – Mullingar

Distance (km): 59

Cycling Time (hours): 2¾–3¼

Grade: 2

Gain: 280m

Score: ✳ ✳ ✳

Traffic: 2

Train Station: Mullingar

Grid Reference: N 433 527

Lilliput on Lough Ennell is where Jonathan Swift is said to have got his inspiration for Gulliver's Travels. The route also passes Lough Owel as it follows parts of designated cycling routes. It returns to Mullingar on the Royal canal towpath.

Lough Owel, County Westmeath.

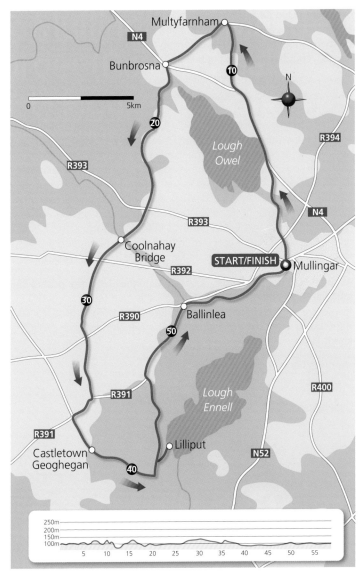

On exiting Mullingar train station car park, turn right to the traffic lights. At the lights go left and then immediately right, following the sign for Longford. At the nearby roundabout take the second exit to another roundabout and then take the first exit. At yet another roundabout, take the second exit and finally at a mini-roundabout take the second exit, signposted for Multyfarnham and Cycle Route 1. Continue out of Mullingar and cycle on to the T-junction at the busy N4. Turn left onto the hard shoulder of the N4, following the signs for Sligo and Cycle Route 1. Lough Owel is next to the road while its views capture the eye.

Around AD 820, the Viking Turgesius came to Ireland with 120 longships and wreaked havoc. He destroyed Irish sacred places and spread fear throughout the country. On the banks of Lough Owel, he built a fortress near the home of the Irish King Malachy. Malachy had a beautiful daughter and Turgesius wanted her as his bride. Malachy was reluctant but did not want to upset the Viking so he hatched a plan. He dispatched his daughter and fifteen armed warriors dressed as women to Turgesius. In the meantime, the Viking had invited fifteen fellow chieftains to his fort, promising each a new bride. They all put their weapons aside, not expecting trouble from the 'women'. When Malachy's daughter and her companions arrived they were taken to individual Viking quarters. In no time Turgesius's fifteen guests were dead and Turgesius made a prisoner. Malachy showed no mercy and had him drowned in Lough Owel.

At about 9km from Mullingar, right turn onto the L1819, signposted for Multyfarnham and Cycle Route 1. Follow this road to the T-junction in the centre of Multyfarnham and turn left towards Bunbrosna. Follow the road to Bunbrosna crossroads at the N4. The distance cycled is about 16km.

Multyfarnham.

Lock 26 on the Royal Canal at Coolnahay.

Multyfarnham is a neat tranquil village and a previous recepient of a Tidy Towns award. The long and narrow Lake Derravaragh nearby is suitable for boating and fishing and is popular with trout and pike anglers. The village is also famous for its Franciscan friary. The friars came here in the thirteenth century at the invitation of the Normans and, though suffering raids and burnings during the sixteenth and seventeenth centuries, the Order persevered to continue their spiritual mission today.

Cross the staggered crossroads at Bunbrosna onto the L1804, keeping left to follow Cycle Route 1. Having cycled about 20km, keep right at a Y-junction onto Cycle Route 2 and leave Route 1 behind. Stay on Cycle Route 2 to reach a crossroads at the R393. Cross the R393 onto the L1804, signposted for Cycle Route 2. Continue to Coolnahay Bridge and cross over the Royal Canal to arrive eventually at a staggered crossroads with the R392. Cross the R392 onto the L5236, signposted for Cycle Route 2 and Castletown Geoghegan. Arrive at another crossroads with the R390. Cross the R390 to continue on the L5236 to a T-junction at the R391, 35km from the start. Turn right onto the R391 and cycle to a crossroads with the R389. Turn left onto this road and continue into Castletown Geoghegan.

Castletown Geoghegan was the seat of the Geoghegan family, who were of ancient Irish lineage and major landholders in Westmeath. One of the more famous was Kedagh Geoghegan. He was renowned for his legendary deeds and, during the anti-Catholic Penal Law period of the eighteenth century, he managed to retain his Catholicism and his landholdings. He also built nearby Jamestown Court around 1720, a fine country house designed in the Palladian style. Much of the stone for the construction may

Lilliput by Lough Ennell.

have been taken from the ancient Geoghegan castle of Carne which stood nearby. Currently Jamestown Court is not open to the public.

Cycle through Castletown Geoghegan and after passing the playground turn left onto the L1120, signposted for Lilliput. Cycle on to the junction signposted for Cycle Route 3 and turn left onto this route. Soon after, divert right to Lilliput and Lough Ennell.

Lilliput got its name after Jonathan Swift published his satirical classic *Gulliver's Travels*. The area was known as Nure before Swift's bestseller. It was said locally that the idea for the little people of fictional Lilliput was based on Swift's viewing of actual people at a distance while he was on Lough Ennell. A scribe of many talents, he may have been the author of an essay called 'The Benefit of Farting Explain'd'. He argues eloquently that many of the 'distempers' affecting the 'fair sex' are due to 'flatulences not adequately vented' – strange musings indeed for a clergyman!

Having returned from Lilliput, turn right to continue on Cycle Route 3. Arrive at a junction with the R391 and turn right onto it, following the sign for Mullingar. The road terminates at a T-junction with the R390 at Ballinea. Turn right onto the R390, signposted for Mullingar and Cycle Routes 2 and 3. On the far side of Ballinea is a right turn onto the cycle track along the Royal Canal into Mullingar. Follow the well-paved track back to the railway station.

25. Mullingar-to-Meath Border (Royal Canal East) Figure of Eight

Mullingar – Belvedere House – Coralstown – Killucan – Mullingar

Distance (km): 57	**Score:** ✳ ✳ ✳
Cycling Time (hours): 3–3½	**Traffic:** 1
Grade: 2	**Train Station:** Mullingar
Gain: 139m	**Grid Reference:** N 433 527

If you are looking for a relaxed, easy cycle, this one is for you. The quiet roads pass through attractive Westmeath countryside and the route follows a section of the Royal Canal east of Mullingar. Belvedere House and Gardens make a pleasant visit.

Jealous Wall at Belvedere House, County Westmeath.

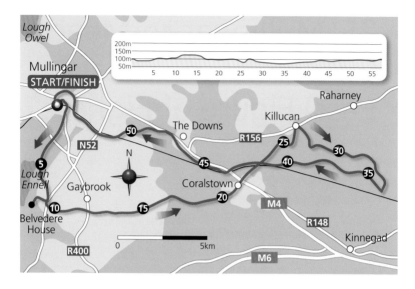

On exiting Mullingar train station car park, cycle to the traffic lights and turn right towards the town centre. Take the second exit at a nearby roundabout and then turn right at the subsequent traffic lights, following the sign for Belvedere House and the N52. Continue on this road, passing through three roundabouts and following the signs for Belvedere House and the N52. The fourth roundabout is called Bloomfield. Take the second exit off it, signposted for Hotel and Cycle Route 3. Cycle past Bloomfield House Hotel and Mullingar Golf Club. The entrance to Belvedere House is after the golf club and about 7km from the start. A diversion to Belvedere House and back is 2km. The house and gardens are open to the public for an entrance fee. There is also a coffee shop.

Robert Rochfort lived in Belvedere House while estranged from his wife, Mary. He had her imprisoned in their previous home at Gaulstown. This was over an alleged affair with his younger brother Arthur. Robert was convinced of his wife's deception and was egged on by another brother, George, who despised Mary. Arthur was put on trial for adultery, resulting in him being made penniless. He was sentenced to eighteen years in debtors' prison. Robert and George then had a falling out after George built a superior house to Belvedere at Tudenham nearby. In a huff, Robert built the 'Jealous Wall' to cut off the view to George's mansion. Robert's son finally freed his mother after his father's death in 1774. By that time she had suffered mentally and physically. On her own deathbed, she swore there was never an affair with Arthur. As you might imagine, the Rochforts' behaviour was one of the great social scandals of the time.

From the entrance to Belvedere House, continue to the nearby junction with the N52 and turn right. Take the next left turn onto the L5136, signposted for Ganestown and Cycle Route 3. The road twists right and then left at a solid little church by a signpost for Cycle Route 3. Continue on Cycle Route 3 to a staggered crossroads by an old hand pump. Cross to the L1005, signposted for Milltownpass, and leave Cycle Route 3 behind. After passing a forest entrance, turn left, following the sign for The Downs. Continue to a staggered crossroads and turn right, which is signposted for Killucan. Cycle to Coralstown where there is fine church.

There was a story told hereabouts of three men in a public house talking about excavations happening in a local cemetery. Two of the men were afraid that the work would disturb the ghosts of the dead, while the third said he didn't believe in ghosts. 'A five pound note says you won't bring back a skull from that cemetery,' says one. 'You're on,' says the non-believer and off he went. Meanwhile, the other two took a shortcut to the cemetery and hid behind a tomb. The non-believer arrived and picked up a skull from a pile dug up during the excavations. 'Put it back, it's my head,' announced a voice from behind the tomb. He put it back and picked up another one. 'Put that back, it's mine,' said another voice from behind the same tomb. After looking nervously around, he quickly picked up a skull and ran off with it shouting, 'It'll be in the pub, if you want it back.' Meanwhile the other two were already in the pub having a good laugh when he walked in and placed the skull on the counter, saying, 'I'll take that fiver.' He had just finished the words when the door burst open. All three looked at the door, but there was nobody there. When they looked back at the counter, the skull was gone. 'It's gone,' gasped the non-believer. Quick as a wink, his friend said, 'I'll take me fiver back so.'

After passing Coralstown, cross over the motorway and follow the signs for Killucan and Rathwire. Cross over the canal and cycle on to a T-junction, 26km from the start. Turn left and continue to another T-junction in Killucan.

About 1860, a landlord at nearby Cookesborough took exception to Killucan crows invading his estate. The eccentric Adolphus Cooke had provided for his own feathery tenants by instructing his workmen to gather twigs and moss for his crows to build their nests. When the crows didn't take up the offer, he instructed his workmen to build the nests for them. As often happened, one of the workman decided to pull his master's leg. He told Adolphus that Killucan crows were flying in to take the nests of his own feathery flock. Cooke decided to go to war and ordered his workmen to adopt whatever means necessary to dispatch the invading crows back to Killucan. It's no wonder his will was challenged after he died.

At the T-junction in Killucan, cycle towards the church facing you and follow the road around to the right. Continue straight to the L1015, signposted for Kinnegad and, after passing through a set of crossroads and a school, take the next left turn. Continue through another crossroads and then take the next right turn into a cul-de-sac. The turn is about 33km from the start. At the end of this road is the Royal Canal.

The Royal Canal is an amenity that provides enjoyable cycling and walking today. However, its past tells a different story. In May 1847 during the Great Famine, about 1,500 hungry souls set out from Strokestown in County Roscommon to trek the 150km-long canal towpath to Dublin. They were the tenants of Major Denis Mahon, who had offered to pay for their emigration to Canada, a convenient way to clear his land of unproductive tenants. They had little choice, as the alternatives were starvation or the workhouse. From Dublin, they sailed to Liverpool and then to Quebec on board four cargo ships, ironically loaded with Irish grain. The ships were unsuitable for carrying passengers and became known as 'coffin ships' as the journey turned into a nightmare. It is estimated that half died before reaching Canadian soil. Eventually, news of the deaths got back to Roscommon and Mahon was shot dead by aggrieved individuals the following November.

At the Royal Canal, turn right onto a grassy track. After 1km, the surface of the track improves. Continue to a canal bridge and cross it to take up the cycling/pedestrian track on the other side. Cycle to Mullingar by following the cycle/pedestrian signs. As soon as the rail track is visible in Mullingar, exit the canal track onto the road and cross it to the station car park.

Royal Canal near Mullingar, County Westmeath

26. Skerries to Bog of the Ring Loop

Skerries – Man of War – Bog of the Ring – Balrothery – Skerries

Distance (km): 28	**Score:** ✳ ✳ ✳
Cycling Time (hours): 1¼–1¾	**Traffic:** 2
Grade: 1	**Train Station:** Skerries
Gain: 198m	**Grid Reference:** O 246 598

Some easy hills, great views and a bog in decline are included on this route. The remains of the great Irish cycling champion Harry Reynolds are interred at Balrothery. Skerries was National Tidy Towns winner in 2016, making it a worthy place to start and finish.

Bog of the Ring, County Dublin.

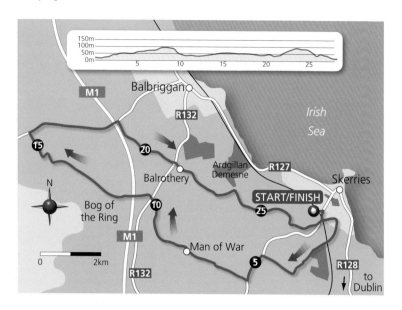

On leaving Skerries train station car park, cycle to the nearby T-junction and turn right, following the sign for Lusk. Continue to the roundabout by the railway tunnel and take the first exit, signposted for Rush. Follow the road to the nearby crossroads and turn right. Cycle on until you reach a staggered crossroads about 3.5km from the railway station. Turn right and continue to a T-junction at the R127. Turn left onto the R127 signposted for Lusk.

Look out for the right-hand turn to the Man of War, about 5.5km from the start. Take this turn and soon you climb a hill. As you ascend there are lovely views to the left of the Dublin and Wicklow mountains. In particular, you should recognise the pimply profile of the Great Sugar Loaf. After topping the hill, there is a descent to the thatched and very old Man of War pub.

In 1810, the travel writer Dr John Gamble wrote that the Man of War Inn was one of the best breakfasting houses. He wrote: 'The bread and butter, tea, sugar and cream were excellent. In this country, 1s 7½d is the regular charge for breakfast and includes everything, eggs, ham etc. In Ireland, toast is rarely brought in swimming in greasy butter, in the disgusting manner too common at an English Inn – it is cut into thin slices, and laid on the table with fresh butter, which everyone puts on for himself.' Sounds very tasty!

The T-junction at the pub is about 8km from Skerries. Turn right here and then left soon after. The road descends to a staggered crossroads

The fifteenth-century church tower at Balrothery, County Dublin.

at the R132. Turn left and then immediately right, following the sign for the Bog of the Ring. Cycle on to cross over the M1 motorway. The Bog of the Ring begins at the Ring Commons Sport Centre on your left. You have covered 12km from the start.

The Bog of the Ring used to be an extensive marshland, but is slowly drying due to its use as a local water supply. Up to four million litres of water is treated daily from the bog; that's a couple of swimming pools worth. It still contains some wet ground where marsh vegetation occurs, but most of the rare plants that were here are gone. Birds, too, have been disturbed. Typical wetlands birds do not breed here. However, the site is used in winter by wetland species such as snipe, golden plover and curlew.

Continue on, passing through a crossroads, to a T-junction connecting with the R122. Turn right onto the R122, signposted for Balbriggan. Cycle on to a roundabout and take the second exit, to cross over the M1 motorway. At the following roundabout, take the second exit also. Soon after, turn right onto the L1125 towards Balrothery, 2km away. Continue to a T-junction at the R132. Turn left and, after the pedestrian lights, right into Balrothery. Turn right again, passing the Balrothery Inn towards the ruined church on a hill. Follow the road to the nearby T-junction and turn right. The entrance to the church is on your right. Balrothery is about 21km from the start.

Near the gable end of the old church is the grave of Harry Reynolds (1874–1940), known as the 'The Balbriggan Flyer'. He wasn't a pilot but a cyclist. He got the name from racing the steam train from Balbriggan to Skerries on his bike. He was Ireland's first world cycling champion, winning in Copenhagen in 1896. When Reynolds was stepping onto the podium to be presented with his medal by the King of Denmark, the band played 'God Save The Queen' and a Union Jack was hoisted. Reynolds was enraged and called the officials, pointing out that he was Irish and would not have his victory accredited to England. The Danes lowered the Union Jack, replacing it with a green flag and the band played an Irish tune.

From the church, continue on to the mini-roundabout and take the first exit, following the sign for Skerries. The distance on the sign is in miles, 4½ (7km). Push a steady climb to a junction and turn left, following the sign for Ardgillan Castle. At the entrance to Ardgillan Castle turn right, following the sign for Skerries Mills, or divert into Ardgillan demesne for magnificent views of the castle and coast. There are tearooms here, too.

In the late eighteenth century, Ardgillan was called Prospect. The house was built about 1738 by Robert Taylor and later inherited by Thomas Taylor, the Earl of Bective. The original house was smaller and devoid of the castellated embellishments there now. Wages for the builders were a penny a day, a bed, a meal and a tot of rough Irish whiskey. The rough whiskey had an edge to cut the dust from the builders' throats.

Having followed the sign for Skerries Mills from Ardgillan Castle, continue past a right-hand turn to descend a hill. As you descend there are fabulous views over the town of Skerries, its islands and Rockabill Lighthouse. Continue to a junction and turn left, following another sign for Skerries Mills. Pass a converted church and soon after descend a short, steep hill to a junction with the R127. Turn left towards the railway tunnel and take the first exit on the roundabout after passing through the tunnel. After a few hundred metres, take the first left back to the railway station.

View of Skerries near Ardgillan Castle, County Dublin.

27. Skerries-to-Castlebellingham Loop

Skerries – Garristown – Castlebellingham – Laytown – Skerries

Distance (km): 131	Score: ✳ ✳ ✳
Cycling Time (hours): 6–7	Traffic: 2
Grade: 4	Train Station: Skerries
Gain: 735m	Grid Reference: O 246 598

This is the longest route in this collection, though it's not very hilly. It has a lovely mix of rural and coastal landscape and plenty of places to stop for refreshments. However, there won't be much time to linger if you want to complete the route in reasonable time.

Garristown, County Dublin.

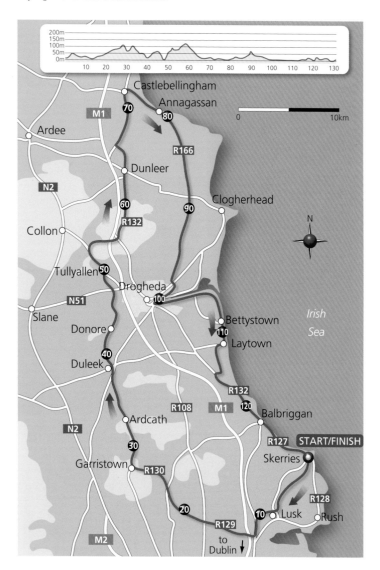

Exit the train station car park and continue to the nearby T-junction. Turn right, following the sign for Lusk. At the nearby roundabout by the railway tunnel, take the first exit, signposted for Rush. Cycle to a crossroads and turn right to leave Skerries behind. Continue on this rural road, passing Skerries Golf Club, to a staggered crossroads and go straight across onto Ballaghstown Lane. Then enjoy the views of Howth and the Dublin and Wicklow mountains ahead.

Continue to a junction about 6km from Skerries and turn left onto Commons Lane. At the nearby T-junction, turn left again onto Raheny Lane. The road eventually terminates at a T-junction at the Lusk ring road near the local schools. Turn right onto the ring road and cycle to a nearby roundabout. Take the first exit into Lusk village and then the first turn right before the pedestrian lights. Continue to the nearby church and turn left before the church. Cycle straight through a crossroads to a T-junction at a builders' providers and turn right.

Continue on this road to T-junction at the R132. Turn left onto the R132, signposted for Swords. After cycling about 13km from the start, take the right-hand turn onto the R129, signposted for Ballyboughal. Continue to the T-junction in Ballyboughal and turn left followed by a right to stay on the R129, signposted for Oldtown and Garristown.

There was a story told hereabouts of a young working-class boy who won a scholarship to a posh boarding school. 'Don't let us down,' were his father's last words when he dropped the boy at school. That evening at communal dinner, the boy began to clean his knife in the tablecloth. The headmaster sitting at the top table noticed. 'Boy,' he called, as the other boys sniggered, 'Would you do that at home?' 'Oh no, sir,' replied the boy, 'we use clean knives at home.'

Near Oldtown, keep to the R129 as it veers right, following the sign for Naul. When the road comes to a staggered crossroads, turn right for Garristown. At around 24km from the start, take the left-hand turn

Obelisk Bridge over the Boyne near Tullyallen, County Louth.

147

onto the R130, signposted for Garristown. Continue to the T-junction in Garristown and turn right onto the L1006, signposted for Duleek.

Cycle through Ardcath, keeping right at a junction in the village. Eventually, arrive at a crossroads at a sign for Duleek. Turn right towards Duleek and continue to a stop sign at a T-junction. Turn right, followed by the next left onto the L16092 into Duleek, about 40km from the start. Follow the road to a T-junction in the village and turn left and then immediately right for Donore. Continue to Donore and at a stop sign in the village, go straight onto the L1601, signposted for Drogheda.

At a nearby thatched cottage, turn left onto L16013, signposted for Tullyallen and the Battle of the Boyne. At the entrance to the Battle of the Boyne site, keep right over the canal bridge and then cross the Obelisk Bridge over the Boyne.

At the end of this bridge on the right is the foundation of a 170ft obelisk that stood here from 1736 to 1923. It was dedicated to William III and his defeat of James II at the Battle of the Boyne in 1690. The obelisk would have dominated the area; however, it was blown up in 1923. The substantial foundation is all that remains.

At the nearby crossroads with the N51, go straight across onto the L2321, which passes through King William's Glen. It is signposted for Tullyallen. At the crossroads in Tullyallen, cycle straight across and continue to a T-junction at the R168. Turn left onto the R168, signposted for Collon.

The Cooley and Mourne mountains viewed from north of Annagassan.

At about 54km, veer right onto the L2299, signposted for Monasterboice. After passing under the M1 motorway, arrive at a T-junction and turn left onto the R132 towards Dunleer. Go right at the next T-junction, following the sign for Dunleer, and then left at another nearby T-junction without signposts. Follow the R132 to Dunleer, passing the Monasterboice dolmen on the way. Cycle through Dunleer and on to Castlebellingham on the R132. In Castlebellingham, turn right onto the R166, signposted for Annagassan. Stay on the R166 to Annagassan and enjoy the views of the Cooley and Mourne mountains.

The longphort or Viking coastal settlement called Linn Duachaill is believed to have been situated to the north of Annagassan. The Vikings are recorded as being settled here in 841, the same year the longphort was founded at Dublin. It was an important site from which raids were launched inland and archaeological evidence seems to support this. Irish metalwork, possibly from ecclesiastical artefacts, has been found and is comparable to artefacts discovered in Viking graves. In 891, the local Irish rose up and forced the Vikings to leave. However, they returned and Linn Duachaill continued as a longphort until around 927 when the site was finally abandoned. Dublin was developing rapidly then and may have overtaken its importance.

Cycle through Annagassan and continue out of the village on the R166, following the signs for Clogherhead. At about 87km from the start, arrive at a stop sign at a crossroads. Cycle straight across onto the L2278, signposted for Sandpit. Continue through Sandpit and cycle to a

Bridge into Annagassan, County Louth.

crossroads at a cemetery. Go straight across onto L2307, signposted for North Quay. Eventually the road comes to a stop sign; keep left towards Baltray Docks and then turn right at the next stop sign nearby. Continue into Drogheda along the north bank of the River Boyne, following the road when it moves away from the river.

Cycle to a crossroads near a pub and turn left, followed by a right onto the docks. Continue to traffic lights at a T-junction in the centre of Drogheda and turn left to cross the river. Then take the first left on the other side by the south bank. At this stage, about 100km has been cycled. Follow the road to Mornington. Continue through Mornington on the R151 to Bettystown and Laytown. Cycle through Laytown to the green railway bridge. Before the railway there is a pedestrian bridge over the River Nanny at a car park. Cross the footbridge and turn right under the railway bridge. Continue on this road to the third right-hand turn and take it. It is about 115km from the start. Cycle to the nearby T-junction. Turn left onto the R132 and keep left on the R132 to avoid the motorway. Follow the road to Balbriggan.

On the way into Balbriggan, the fine edifice of Bremore Castle dominates the view to the left. It is currently under refurbishment. The castle once belonged to the estate of Lord Shelburne, William Petty-FitzMaurice. Born in Dublin, he was British Prime Minister during the final months of the American War of Independence. Unpopular in parliament, he lost his job as prime minister in 1783 after only a year in office. Shelburne's legacy is negotiating the peace that ended the American War. However, the terms were seen as too generous to the Americans and helped his opponents engineer his demise as prime minister. He took little part in public life afterwards and died in 1805.

Cycle into the centre of Balbriggan and turn left onto Quay Street before pedestrian lights. Under the viaduct keep right and follow the road to Skerries, the R127. The coastal views are super. In Skerries, arrive at traffic lights at a T-junction. Turn right, following the signposts for Lusk and the train station. Continue up a hill, passing a petrol station. At the top of the hill, turn right to the train station. It is signposted.

28. Skerries-to-Donabate Loop

Skerries – Loughshinny – Donabate – Man of War – Skerries

Distance (km): 54	Score: ✴ ✴ ✴
Cycling Time (hours): 2½–3	Traffic: 2
Grade: 2	Train Station: Skerries
Gain: 190m	Grid Reference: O 246 598

A varied route that contrasts busy Fingal with its peaceful tranquillity. There are splendid sea and estuary views and wildlife abounds on Malahide Estuary. Newbridge House and its demesne are very popular with visitors and locals alike.

Malahide Estuary, County Dublin.

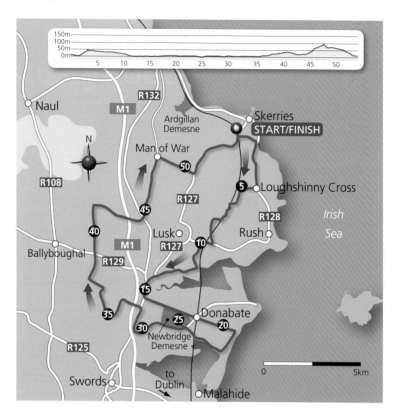

Exit Skerries train station car park and continue to the nearby T-junction. Turn right, following the sign for Lusk. At the nearby roundabout by the railway tunnel, take the first exit, signposted for Rush. Cycle through a crossroads and continue to the T-junction by the coast where the three Skerries Islands face you. Turn right out of the town towards Rush. There is a steady climb for about 2km, then descend to Loughshinny.

At the crossroads in Loughshinny, turn right, following the sign for Lusk. Continue to the first left turn and take it onto Featherbed Lane, about 5km from Skerries. This rural road twists its way to a Y-junction; keep left here, following the sign for Rush. After crossing the railway line, arrive at a T-junction. Turn right, signposted for Swords. Cross the railway line again and soon after, turn left onto the L12801 towards Balleally. This road is called Rogerstown Lane.

The four islands off Skerries are important wildlife sanctuaries that have been designated Special Areas of Protection and Conservation. Rockabill is the furthest offshore and consists of two huge rocks, with a lighthouse perched on the larger one. Rockabill supports the biggest breeding colony of roseate terns in north-west Europe. The birds remain on the island from April to September when they return to winter in Africa. St Patrick's Island, recognisable by the small ruins of a church, supports a large population of breeding cormorants. These dark, long-necked birds can be seen on rocks with wings outstretched. Grey seals also occupy St Patrick's Island. They often follow kayakers and pop up from behind with a loud snort every now and again. Colt is the nearest and smallest island and supports breeding mallard, shelduck, eider duck and ringed plover. The fourth and largest island is Shenick, with its Martello tower. It is tidal and provides sanctuary for birds such as brent geese, curlew and oystercatcher. The islands also serve to enhance the natural beauty of Skerries.

Follow Rogerstown Lane and the mound of Balleally tip head will appear. It looks like a natural hill, but underneath is quite different. The road ends at a T-junction; turn right onto a road with traffic humps. At the end of it is another T-junction. Turn left onto the R127, signposted for Swords. At the nearby junction at Blake's Cross, turn left onto the busy R132, signposted for Dublin. Soon after, and before a large factory-like building, turn left onto Turvey Avenue. Continue to a nearby junction and keep left.

Newbridge House.

Cycle on to enjoy the pleasant tree-lined avenue to Donabate. Enter the town centre at a T-junction and veer left. Cross the railway line and at the nearby cemetery, turn right onto the L2170, signposted for Corballis. Continue to a roundabout and take the third exit to pass Corballis and Balcarrick golf clubs. At this stage, cycling distance is about 20km from the start. Eventually, the road follows the shore of Malahide Estuary, though it is actually the estuary of the Broadmeadow River. The extensive salt marshes and mudflats attract a large population of waterfowl. Continue to the end of the road at an entrance to Newbridge House and demesne. Divert to visit the eighteenth-century house and perhaps have a coffee.

The original owners of Newbridge House were the Cobbes and one of the more curious members of the family was Frances Cobbe, a formidable Victorian woman. She was influential in the women's movement of the nineteenth century. During the period, the woman's place was to be at home looking after her husband and children and generally being a beacon of domestic bliss. She was encouraged to stay out of politics and economics, the domain of men. However, Frances Cobbe rejected this model of inequality. She chose not to conform and rejected marriage. Cobbe argued that women should have control of their own property, seek protection from abusive husbands and participate in the political process. However, she was a paradox. She declined to nominate the married physician Anna Kingsford for membership of a London women's club. Cobbe refused because she believed Kingsford had adopted a profession and career that were incompatible with her domestic duties. It seems that prudish Victorian principles got the better of her.

To continue on the route, turn left while facing the entrance to Newbridge Demesne. Pass a second entrance to the demesne and continue to a large roundabout. Before the roundabout, there is a cycle track on the left by pedestrian lights. Take the track and on descending the short hill, take the tunnel to the right under the roundabout. Exit on the other side to another pedestrian lights. Use this to cross the busy R132 dual carriageway and then turn right, keeping to the hard shoulder. Continue to a roundabout and take the first exit onto a quiet local road, following a sign for Balheary. Total distance cycled is about 30km.

Follow the road to a stop sign at a T-junction and turn right. A peaceful cycle follows through a seasonal canopy, compliments of the trees lining the route, though the quality of the road is questionable. Eventually, arrive at a staggered crossroads, turn right and pass a grass-strip airfield to a crossroads with the R129. Cycle across and continue. The road ends at a T-junction facing a house with a large gate. Turn

The back of the Man of War pub, County Dublin.

right and continue to the T-junction with the R132. Turn left towards Balbriggan and very soon after, take a right off the R132 onto the L1155, signposted to the Man of War pub.

About 500 metres beyond this junction and on the right are the remains of Balrothery workhouse; there is a plaque at a field entrance to mark it. The workhouse system was an undignified solution for desperate people. During the Great Famine the Balrothery workhouse, designed for 400, accommodated about twice that. A 48-bed fever hospital was added to cope. Its burial ground across the road at the back of a nearby field is testimony to the number of people who died, many alone without a loved one: 'Rattle his bones over the stones; he's only a pauper whom nobody owns' (from the nineteenth-century poem 'The Pauper's Drive' by Thomas Noel). However, conditions improved in the 1880s when Thomas and Jane Duffy took over. They reformed the place, replacing straw and cold floors with beds and installed proper toilets and washrooms. The workhouse continued until 1925 when it closed, ending a dark period of local history.

Follow the L1155 uphill to the thatched Man of War pub and turn right. After a short climb, enjoy the views of the Dublin and Wicklow mountains and Lambay Island. Descend and continue to a T-junction with the R127. Turn left onto the R127, signposted for Skerries. On the outskirts of Skerries, pass under the railway tunnel and take the first exit off the roundabout. Continue to the first left-hand turn and take it back to the train station.

29. Skerries-to-Rogerstown Estuary Loop

Skerries – Loughshinny – Rush – Rogerstown – Skerries

Distance (km): 24	**Score:** ✳ ✳ ✳
Cycling Time (hours): 1–1½	**Traffic:** 2
Grade: 1	**Train Station:** Skerries
Gain: 152m	**Grid Reference:** O 246 598

Rogerstown Estuary is one of the most important sanctuaries on the east coast for wintering waders and wildfowl. The route there and back is a mix of coastal and rural charm. Quaint Loughshinny Bay is well worth the visit.

Roundabout at the tunnel under the railway at Skerries, County Dublin.

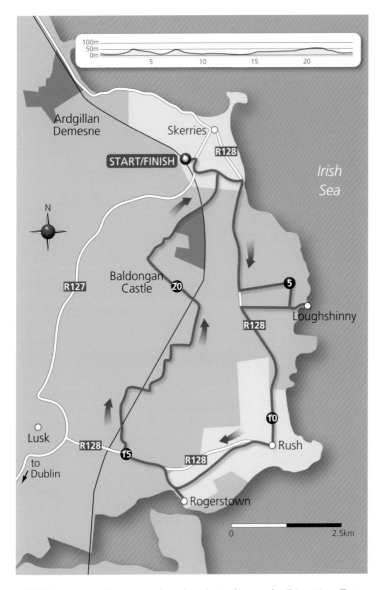

Exit the train station car park and cycle to the nearby T-junction. Turn right, following the sign for Lusk. Continue to the roundabout at the railway tunnel and take the first exit, signposted for Rush. Cycle to the coast road, passing through crossroads on the way. Pause at the T-junction at the coast road to view the Skerries Islands.

Loughshinny Pier.

From right to left, the islands are Shenick with the Martello tower, St Patrick's and Colt. There was once a monastery on St Patrick's Island founded by the saint himself. After his time, the pope thought the Irish were losing the run of themselves and a synod was held to settle it. Fifteen bishops, 200 priests and other clergy attended. How they all managed on that small island was a miracle in itself. Anyway, the pope got his way.

Turn right at the coast onto R128, signposted for Rush. The road ascends eventually to the top of a hill. On descending, pass a 50km speed limit. Take the next left onto a local road and follow it until you come to a T-junction at a thatched cottage. Turn left towards the quaint bay and harbour of Loughshinny. At the harbour, the distance from Skerries is 6km.

The large island off the pier is Lambay, home to Lord Revelstoke. The cliff area opposite the pier is Drumanagh where the Martello tower is located. There is evidence of an Iron Age promontory fort on the site. Roman artefacts were found that suggest the Romans were here. It's a pity they didn't stay because their brilliant engineers might have built us a decent water and sewage system.

Cycle back from the harbour and go straight on at the junction by the thatched cottage. Continue to the top of the road at the staggered crossroads of Loughshinny Cross. Turn left onto the R128 towards Rush and while descending the hill enjoy the view of Lambay Island. At the signalled T-junction in the centre of Rush, turn right. Continue along the main street to the Y-junction past pedestrian lights at a supermarket. Keep left at the junction onto the L1310, signposted for Rogerstown. The L1310 is known locally as the Channel Road. Continue on the Channel Road to a junction at Rogerstown Estuary. The total distance to the estuary is 13km.

Rogerstown is where birds come on holiday and is a feathery melting pot popular with birdwatchers. From autumn through winter and early spring, the estuary is home to large numbers of wildfowl including greylag, brent goose, shelduck, wigeon, teal, shoveler, goldeneye and red-breasted merganser. It also attracts little egret and birds of prey like buzzard, sparrowhawk, peregrine and kestrel. Waders found include golden plover, grey plover, lapwing, knot, dunlin, black-tailed godwit, curlew, redshank and greenshank. In autumn, little stint, curlew, sandpiper and ruff can be seen. The nearby refuse dump at Balleally attracts large numbers of noisy gulls to add to the winged chorus.

Turn right at the aforesaid junction and follow the L1276 to a T-junction with an old mill opposite. Turn left onto the R128 in the direction of Lusk. At a total distance of about 15km, there is a bus stop. Take the next right onto a local road after the bus stop. This road is secluded and easily missed. (If Lusk/Rush train station comes into view, the turn has been missed.) Follow the local road and after crossing the railway track,

Rogerstown Estuary.

The fifteenth-century church at Baldongan near Skerries.

arrive at a Y-junction. Keep right in the direction of Loughshinny. Follow this meandering road crossing the railway track once more. After a total distance of 19km, arrive at a T-junction. Turn left and cross the railway again. The road rises towards Baldongan Castle on the left.

The castle is gone now and what remains on the site is a church built in the fifteenth century. The castle itself was constructed in the thirteenth century and was rectangular with towers at each corner. It was the home of the de Bermingham and later the Barnwell families. In 1649, Irish anti-Parliamentarians held the castle. It was pounded into submission by Cromwellian artillery and the 200-strong garrison was massacred. Because of this and other atrocities, Cromwell will never be the darling of Irish history. The English weren't too fond of him either. On the restoration of Charles II, Cromwell's exhumed body was hung in chains for most of the day and then his head was placed on a 20ft spike.

From the castle, descend the short hill to a crossroads and turn right. Follow this twisting road and look out for the Mourne Mountains in the distance. Pass Skerries Golf Club and cross the railway line again, eventually reaching the outskirts of Skerries. The larger of the two Skerries windmills comes into view here. Arrive at a crossroads and turn left following the sign for Dublin. Follow the road to the roundabout at the railway tunnel. Take the second exit and after a few hundred metres, turn left to return to the railway station.